BOOKS 1 & 2
COMBO EDITION

T0086994

HAL LEONARD
BASS
TAB METHOD

Written by Eric W. Wills

Contributing Editors: Kurt Plahna, Jeff Schroedl, and Jim Schustedt

To access audio visit:
www.halleonard.com/mylibrary

"Enter Code"
4824-4217-6911-1443

ISBN 978-1-70514-172-4

Visit Hal Leonard Online at
www.halleonard.com

Contact us:
Hal Leonard
7777 West Bluemound Road
Milwaukee, WI 53213
Email: info@halleonard.com

In Europe, contact:
Hal Leonard Europe Limited
42 Wigmore Street
Marylebone, London, W1U 2RN
Email: info@halleonardeurope.com

In Australia, contact:
Hal Leonard Australia Pty. Ltd.
4 Lentara Court
Cheltenham, Victoria, 3192 Australia
Email: info@halleonard.com.au

GETTING STARTED

PARTS OF THE BASS GUITAR

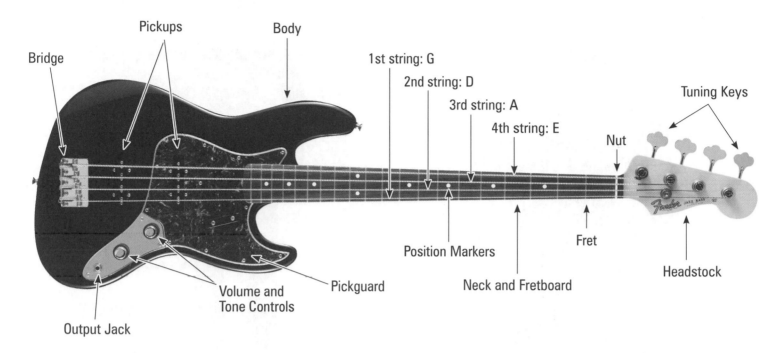

Bridge

Pickups

Body

1st string: G

2nd string: D

3rd string: A

4th string: E

Tuning Keys

Nut

Output Jack

Volume and
Tone Controls

Pickguard

Position Markers

Neck and Fretboard

Fret

Headstock

THE BASS AMP

To hear yourself clearly, it is necessary to play the electric bass through an amplifier. Amps come in a wide range of sizes, but a simple, small unit like the one pictured here will work well. With the amplifier off, plug one end of an instrument cable, or "patch cord," into the bass and the other end into the input jack on the amp. Next, make sure the amp's volume is all the way down and the tone controls are set at 12 o'clock. Now turn the unit on and slowly raise the volume knob while plucking an open string until the right volume level is achieved.

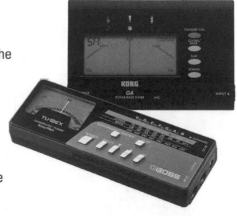

TUNING

The quickest and most accurate way to get in tune is to use an electronic tuner. The four open strings on a bass should be tuned to these pitches:

E (thickest)–A–D–G (thinnest)

To tune your bass, adjust the tuning keys on the headstock. Tightening a key will raise the pitch of a string; loosening a key will lower the pitch. It's important to turn the keys slowly
so that you don't overshoot your mark.

After plugging in to the tuner, make sure the volume control on the bass is turned (clockwise) all the way up. Starting with the high G, strike the open string and adjust the tuning key until the tuner's meter indicates that the pitch is correct. Follow the same process with the D, A, and E strings. Or, listen to each string's correct pitch on track 1 and turn the tuning key until the sound of the string matches the sound on the track.

HOLDING THE BASS

Use the pictures below to help find a comfortable playing position. Whether you decide to sit or stand, it's important to remain relaxed and tension-free.

LEFT-HAND POSITION

Fingers are numbered 1 through 4. Arch your fingers and press the strings down firmly between the frets with your fingertips only.

Place your thumb on the underside of the bass guitar neck. Avoid letting the palm of your hand touch the neck.

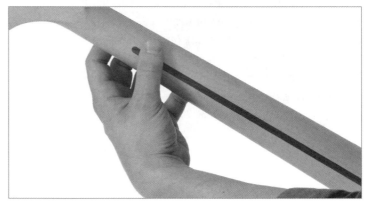

RIGHT-HAND POSITION

Rest your thumb on top of the pickup of the bass and let your fingers hang down loosely over the strings. Use your index and middle fingers alternately to pluck the strings upward, coming to rest on your thumb.

THE E STRING

Bass guitar music is written in a form of notation called **tablature**, or **tab** for short. Each horizontal line represents a string, and each number represents a fret. The thickest string played open, or not pressed, is the low E note. In tab, an open string is represented with a zero (0). The note F is located on the 1st fret. Press, or "fret" the string with your 1st finger, directly behind the first metal fret.

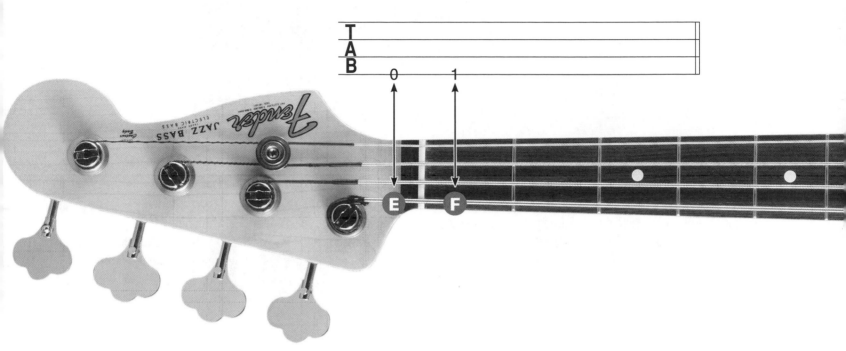

GETTING THE FEEL 🔊

Begin by playing only open E notes. Place the pad of your picking-hand index finger on the E string, press down lightly, and drag it across to your thumb, allowing the string to ring out. Next, use your middle finger to pluck the string in the same fashion. Continue to alternate between these two fingers until it feels natural.

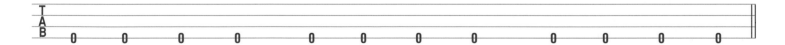

THEME FROM "JAWS" 🔊

Play the theme from the movie *Jaws* using the notes E and F. To get a good sound from the F, make sure your 1st finger presses down just behind (not on top of) the 1st fret. Alternate your picking fingers as in the last exercise. Speed up as the numbers get closer together.

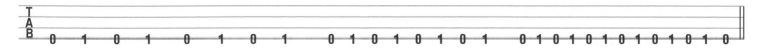

By John Williams
Copyright © 1975 USI B MUSIC PUBLISHING
Copyright Renewed
All Rights Controlled and Administered by SONGS OF UNIVERSAL, INC

Now let's learn more notes on the E string.

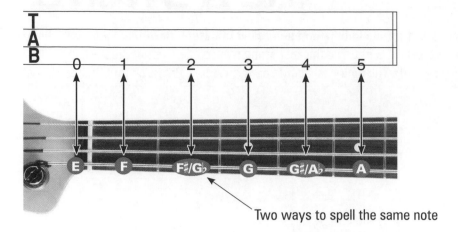

Two ways to spell the same note

GREEN ONIONS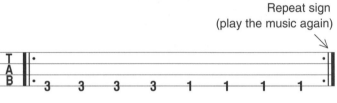

"Green Onions" by Booker T. & the MG's uses the notes E, G, and A. Follow the tab and play the notes at a steady speed, or **tempo**. Use your 1st finger to fret the G note and 4th finger to fret the A.

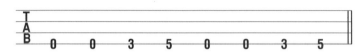

MY GENERATION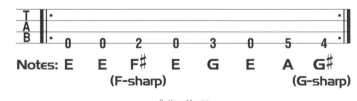

"My Generation" by the Who begins with this two-note phrase. Use your 1st finger to fret F and 4th finger for G. The **repeat signs** tell you to play the music again. Practice this example slowly and steadily at first before increasing the tempo.

Repeat sign
(play the music again)

STRAY CAT STRUT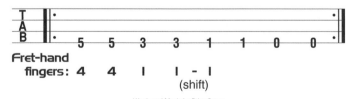

Besides the famous song by the Stray Cats, this bass line has been used in many tunes. "Hit the Road Jack" by Ray Charles is one example. Begin with your 4th finger on A. After playing the second G note with your 1st finger, you'll have to shift your fret hand down to play the F with your 1st finger.

Fret-hand
fingers: 4   4   I   I - I
              (shift)

PETER GUNN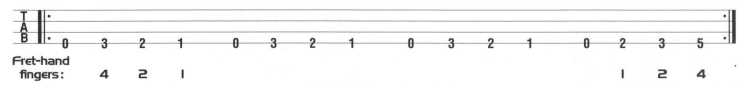

A **riff** is a short, composed phrase that is repeated. The popular riff from "Peter Gunn" is played with notes on the low E string.

Notes: E   E   F#   E   G   E   A   G#
              (F-sharp)   (G-sharp)

FOR WHOM THE BELL TOLLS 🔊

Whenever you play a span of three consecutive frets on the lower portion of the bass neck (first five frets), use only your 1st, 2nd, and 4th fret-hand fingers. Skipping the 3rd finger will limit tension in your hand and wrist.

Fret-hand
fingers: 4   2   1   1   2   4

THE A STRING

Here are the notes within the first five frets of the 3rd string, called the A string.

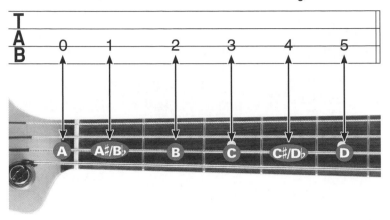

BRIT ROCK

This catchy riff uses the notes A, B, and C. To get the best sound from any note on the A string, pluck the string, letting your picking finger come to rest against the E string.

LEAN ON ME

This song was a #1 hit in two decades. It uses the notes A, B, C♯, and D. There are a few correct ways to finger this riff with your fret hand, but the one written below works well with minimal hand strain.

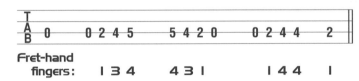

Fret-hand fingers: 1 3 4   4 3 1   1 4 4 1

RHYTHM TAB

Rhythm tab adds rhythmic values to the basic tab staff. **Bar lines** divide music into **measures**. A **time signature** tells how many beats are in each measure and what kind of note is counted as one beat. In 4/4 time ("four-four"), there are four beats in each measure, and a **quarter note** is counted as one beat. It has a vertical stem joined to the tab number.

FEEL THE BEAT

Count "1, 2, 3, 4" as you play.

Quarter-note stem

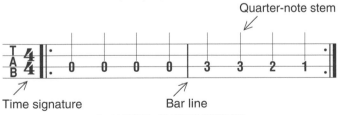

Time signature   Bar line

LADY MADONNA

This classic riff by the Beatles uses quarter notes on strings 3 and 4.

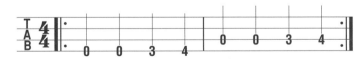

ZEPPELIN TRIBUTE

Make sure your thumb is anchored on the pickup for picking-hand stability.

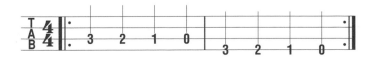

BLUES RIFF

Moving from B with your 1st finger to C♯ with your 3rd can be a bit of a stretch for your hand. To minimize strain, quickly shift your hand up the neck after playing B to get in position for the following note.

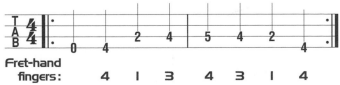

Fret-hand fingers: 4 1 3   4 3 1 4

MORE RIFFS

The next two riffs are written in **3/4 time**. This means there are three beats in each measure, and a quarter note receives one beat.

MY NAME IS JONAS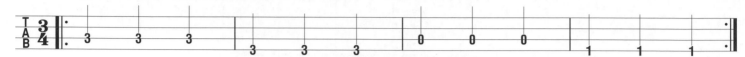

Count "1–2–3, 1–2–3" as you play this riff by the band Weezer.

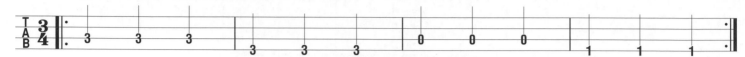

Words and Music by Rivers Cuomo, Patrick Wilson and Jason Cropper
Copyright © 1994 E.O. Smith Music, Fie! and Ubermommasuprapoppa Music
All Rights for E.O. Smith Music and Fie! Administered by Wixen Music Publishing, Inc.

MALAGUEÑA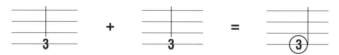

This traditional Spanish piece is very popular among classical guitarists.

By Francisco Tarrega
Copyright © 2013 by HAL LEONARD CORPORATION

A **half note** lasts two beats. It fills the time of two quarter notes. In tab, a circle surrounds the tab number(s) and is attached to a vertical stem.

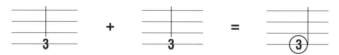

CANON IN D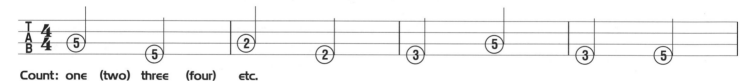

The first line is played with half notes and the second line is played with quarter notes. Count aloud and keep a steady tempo.

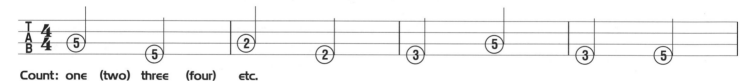

Count: one (two) three (four) etc.

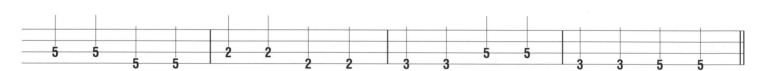

By Johann Pachelbel
Copyright © 2013 by HAL LEONARD CORPORATION

ELECTRIC FUNERAL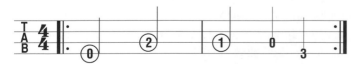

The heavy metal band Black Sabbath used half notes and quarter notes for this powerful, eerie riff.

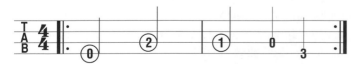

Words and Music by Frank Iommi, John Osbourne, William Ward and Terence Butler
© Copyright 1970 (Renewed) and 1974 (Renewed) Onward Music Ltd., London, England
TRO - Essex Music International, Inc., New York, controls all publication rights for the U.S.A. and Canada

ALL BLUES

Now try playing half notes in 3/4 time.

By Miles Davis
Copyright © 1959 JAZZ HORN MUSIC CORP.
Copyright Renewed
All Rights Controlled and Administered by SONGS OF UNIVERSAL, INC.

An **eighth note** lasts half a beat, or half as long as a quarter note. One eighth note is written with a stem and flag; consecutive eighth notes are connected with a beam.

WITH OR WITHOUT YOU

This classic song by U2 has a repetitive, eighth-note bass line. When counting eighth notes, use the word "and" between the beats—1 and 2 and 3 and 4 and. The numbers are called **downbeats** and each "and" is called an **upbeat**.

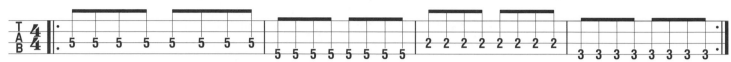

Count: one and two and three and four and

AQUALUNG

Now let's mix eighth notes and quarter notes on this famous Jethro Tull song.

GREEN-EYED LADY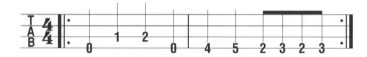

Experiment to determine which fingers work best for this classic Sugarloaf riff.

A **rest** is a symbol used to indicate silence in music. In 4/4 time, a **quarter rest** fills the time of one beat and a **half rest** fills the time of two beats.

Quarter Rest	Half Rest
𝄽	▬
One Beat	Two Beats

25 OR 6 TO 4

This riff by the band Chicago uses a quarter rest. Mute the string by touching it with the tip of your picking finger. You can also release the pressure of your fret hand to silence the string.

Count: one and two and three (four)

BRAIN STEW

The band Green Day used a similar descending pattern for this hit song, which uses quarter and half rests.

Count: one and (two) (three - four)

THE D STRING

Here are the notes within the first five frets of the 2nd string, called the D string.

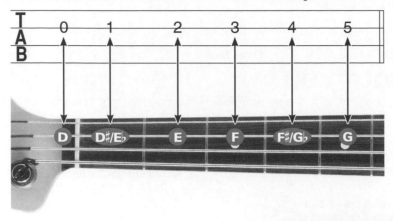

D-MENTED

When playing multiple notes on the D string, you should move your picking-hand thumb, which was resting on the pickup, to the E string as pictured to the right. This move will help you to reach the D string more easily with your picking fingers. Say the notes out loud as you play this riff.

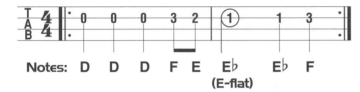

Notes: D   D   D   F   E   E♭   E♭   F
                         (E-flat)

MACHINE GUN

Jimi Hendrix used this riff as the foundation for his song from the album *Band of Gypsys*.

Words and Music by Jimi Hendrix
Copyright © 1970 by EXPERIENCE HENDRIX, L.L.C.
Copyright Renewed 1998
All Rights Controlled and Administered by EXPERIENCE HENDRIX, L.L.C.

BILLIE JEAN

Notice the fret-hand fingering from F♯ to C♯ in this Michael Jackson hit. The transition from a higher to lower string on the same fret can be made smoother by using two fingers as written here. Rest your thumb on the E string throughout this riff.

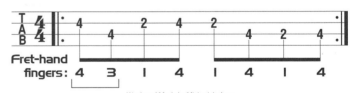

Fret-hand fingers: 4 3   1 4   1 4 1   4

Words and Music by Michael Jackson
Copyright © 1982 Mijac Music
All Rights Administered by Sony/ATV Music Publishing LLC, 8 Music Square West, Nashville, TN 37203

YOU GIVE LOVE A BAD NAME

Use the same type of fingering pattern across the A and E strings here that you did in "Billie Jean."

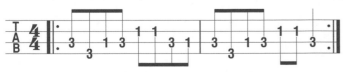

Words and Music by Jon Bon Jovi, Desmond Child and Richie Sambora
Copyright © 1986 UNIVERSAL - POLYGRAM INTERNATIONAL PUBLISHING, INC., BON JOVI PUBLISHING,
SONY/ATV MUSIC PUBLISHING LLC and AGGRESSIVE MUSIC
All Rights for BON JOVI PUBLISHING Controlled and Administered by UNIVERSAL -
POLYGRAM INTERNATIONAL PUBLISHING, INC.
All Rights for SONY/ATV MUSIC PUBLISHING LLC and AGGRESSIVE MUSIC Administered by SONY/ATV MUSIC
PUBLISHING LLC, 8 Music Square West, Nashville, TN 37203

AUTHORITY SONG

Begin with your picking-hand thumb resting on the E string to play the notes on the D string. Then shift your thumb to the pickup for the rest of the riff. Skipping the A string makes this bass line tricky, so practice slowly.

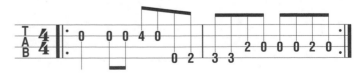

Words and Music by John Mellencamp
© 1983 EMI FULL KEEL MUSIC

A **tie** is a curved, dashed line connecting two notes of the same pitch. It tells you not to strike the second note. The first note should be struck and held for the combined value of both notes.

Two Beats   Three Beats   One Beat

TIE IT DOWN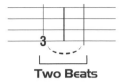

The tie in this riff connects a quarter note on beat 4 to a quarter note on beat 1 of the next measure. Count as you play.

Count: one (two) three four (one) two three four

I HEARD IT THROUGH
THE GRAPEVINE

There are two different ties in this Motown bass riff. The second one that happens ties the "and" of beat 3 to beat 4, lasting one and a half beats total. Listen to the audio example for reference.

Count: one two and three four (one) two and three and (four)

(SITTIN' ON) THE DOCK OF THE BAY

This recognizable bass line from Otis Redding's #1 hit song connects the last eighth note of one measure to a **whole note** in the following measure. A whole note lasts four beats.

Whole note

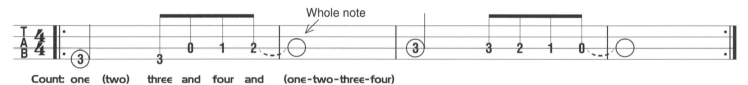

Count: one (two) three and four and (one-two-three-four)

SPACE TRUCKIN'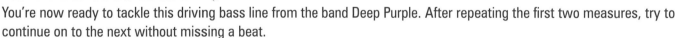

You're now ready to tackle this driving bass line from the band Deep Purple. After repeating the first two measures, try to continue on to the next without missing a beat.

An **eighth rest** indicates to be silent for half a beat. It looks like this: 𝄾

HAVA NAGILA (LET'S BE HAPPY) 🔊

Start slowly and use your pinky for the G♯ on the 4th fret.

Count: one   two (three) and four and

PORK AND BEANS 🔊

This repeating riff is a prominent part in one of Weezer's biggest hits.

Count: one   (two)   and   three   four

CROSSFIRE 🔊

The legendary Stevie Ray Vaughan recorded this song which is anchored by a hard-hitting bass line.

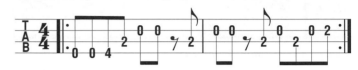

A **staccato** mark looks like a dot written above or below a note. It indicates that the note it is attached to should be played shorter than normal, and can be an important component to the feel of a bass line.

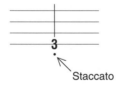

Staccato

SUPER FREAK 🔊

This funky Rick James hit uses both eighth and quarter rests.

PUMP IT UP 🔊

Here's the intro riff to a song by Elvis Costello. To get the staccato notes short, release the pressure of your fret hand from the note, as you would for a rest.

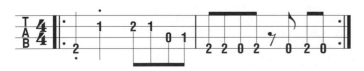

LOUIE, LOUIE 🔊

Use your fret hand to stop the sound of an open string for a rest or staccato note by lightly placing it on top of the strings.

A special technique for the fret hand is the **finger roll**. This is helpful when you need to quickly and smoothly move between two notes on adjacent strings that are on the same fret. To do this when moving from a lower to a higher string, play the note on the lower string with the tip of your finger and your knuckle slightly bent [Photo 1]. Then flatten the knuckle and roll your finger to the next string, playing the note on the higher string with the pad of your finger [Photo 2]. Reverse the sequence when rolling from a higher to a lower string.

Photo 1

Photo 2

DAY TRIPPER

On this Beatles classic, roll from the 3rd to the 2nd string using your index finger.

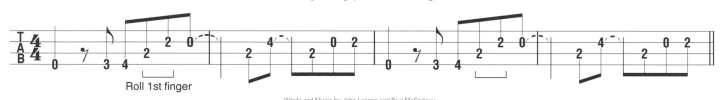

Roll 1st finger

JAZZY

Begin this jazz-style bass line with your 4th finger on the third fret. Then use your 2nd finger to roll across the two notes on the second fret.

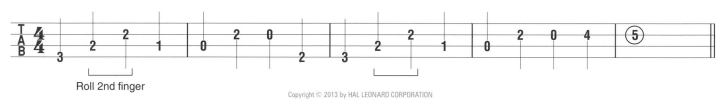

Roll 2nd finger

The next riffs begin with **pickup notes**. Count pickup notes as if they were the last portion of a full measure.

YOU REALLY GOT ME

Van Halen covered this Kinks song on their first album.

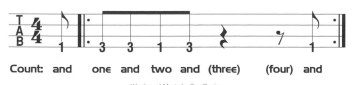

Count: and   one   and   two   and   (three)   (four)   and

MISSISSIPPI QUEEN

The intro to this song by the band Mountain has a one-and-a-half beat pickup.

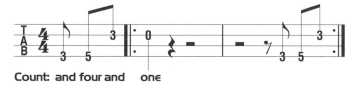

Count: and four and   one

ALL THE SMALL THINGS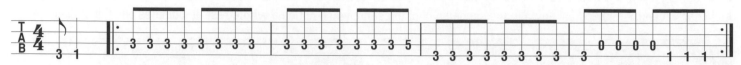

This song by Blink-182 opens with a fast, driving bass line. Play the C notes with your 1st finger so you can reach the D with your 4th.

I WALK THE LINE

There's a three-beat pickup in the intro to this famous Johnny Cash song. The **fermata** sign above the last note of the song tells you to hold the note longer than its normal value to create a nice ending. Fermatas are also used within songs to create a pause in the music.

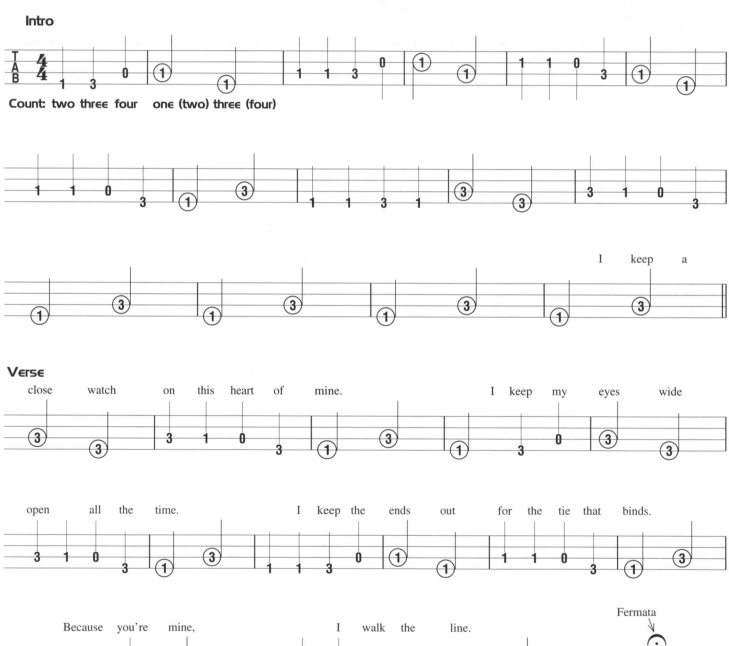

WIPE OUT

It's time to play your first complete song. "Wipe Out" is one of the most popular instrumental hits of all time. It was originally recorded by the Surfaris in 1963 and has been performed since by numerous groups, including the Ventures and the Beach Boys.

During the famous drum breakdown in the second half of the song, you'll notice a **whole rest**. It indicates one full measure of silence, and looks like this: ▬

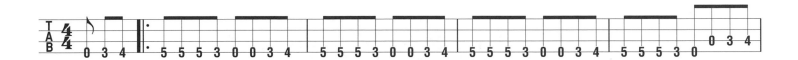

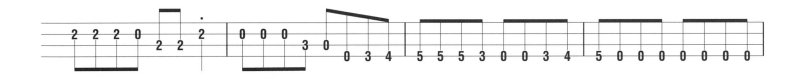

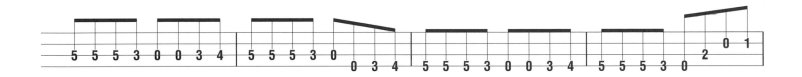

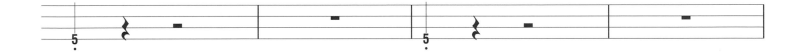

By The Surfaris
© 1963 (Renewed) MIRALESTE MUSIC and ROBIN HOOD MUSIC CO.

THE G STRING

Here are the notes within the first five frets of the 1st string, called the G string.

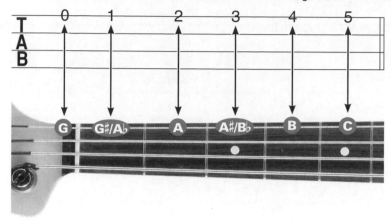

EVERY BREATH YOU TAKE 🔊

Play the melody to this hit pop song by the Police.

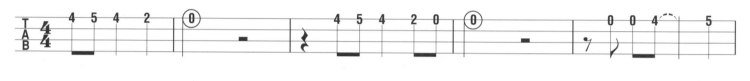

STAND BY ME 🔊

The bass line to this timeless classic by Ben E. King was originally played on the upright bass, but it sounds just as great on the electric.

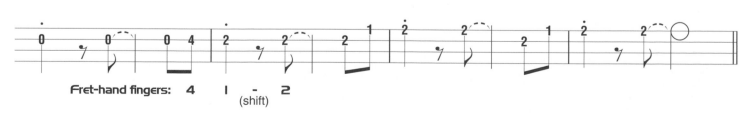

Fret-hand fingers: 4 1 - 2
(shift)

When a **dot** appears after a note, you extend the note by half its value. A **dotted half note** lasts for three beats.

BABA O'RILEY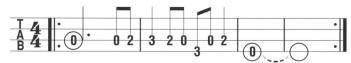

This classic rock riff by the Who has a dotted half note.

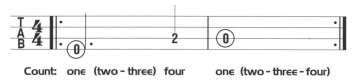

Count: one (two - three) four   one (two - three - four)

THE CHAIN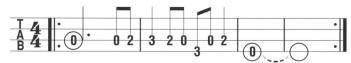

The famous breakdown in this Fleetwood Mac song features the bass player.

NORWEGIAN WOOD (THIS BIRD HAS FLOWN)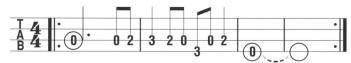

Play the melody to this Indian-influenced Beatles song in 3/4 time. Here, the dotted half note equals one whole measure.

RAKE TECHNIQUE

When moving from a high string to a lower one, use the same picking finger to play both strings—this is called the **rake technique**. This will allow you to keep your picking hand relaxed and play with less overall effort. The following examples illustrate when to use your index finger (i) or middle finger (m).

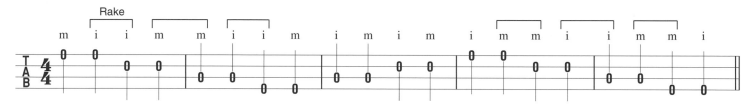

I CAN'T HELP MYSELF
(SUGAR PIE, HONEY BUNCH)

This Motown bass line was recorded by the great James Jamerson for the Four Tops. The fingering (rake) pattern reverses every measure.

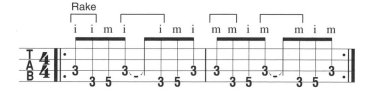

WE GOTTA GET OUT
OF THIS PLACE

Use your 1st finger (fret hand) to roll from F down to C in this riff by the Animals. The roll should be executed starting with the pad of your finger on F and moving toward the tip for C.

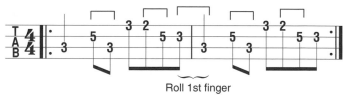

Roll 1st finger

CHECKPOINT

You're halfway through this book and well on your way to a rewarding hobby or a successful career with the electric bass guitar. Let's take a moment to review some of what you've learned so far.

NOTE NAMES

Draw a line to match each note on the left with its correct name on the right.

    C

    B

    G

    E

    F

    A

    D

SYMBOLS & TERMS

Draw a line to match each symbol on the left with its correct name on the right.

    Time Signature

   Half Note

Eighth Rest

    Quarter Rest

    Eighth Note

    Repeat Sign

Half Rest

Write the note names in the spaces provided.

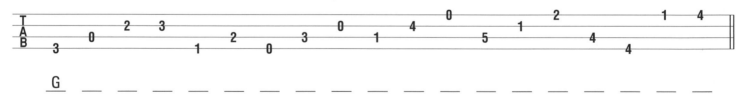

G _ _ _ _ _ _ _ _ _ _ _ _ _ _ _

Add bar lines.

Below the tab staff are note names. Write the notes on the tab staff.

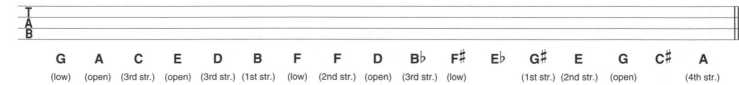

G	A	C	E	D	B	F	F	D	Bb	F#	Eb	G#	E	G	C#	A
(low)	(open)	(3rd str.)	(open)	(3rd str.)	(1st str.)	(low)	(2nd str.)	(open)	(3rd str.)	(low)		(1st str.)	(2nd str.)	(open)		(4th str.)

SIGNED, SEALED, DELIVERED I'M YOURS

This Stevie Wonder song features a bass line by legendary bassist James Jamerson. The verse section is tabbed with **ending brackets**. On the first time through, play the 1st ending and repeat back to the beginning of the verse. The second time, skip the 1st ending and play the 2nd ending.

Intro

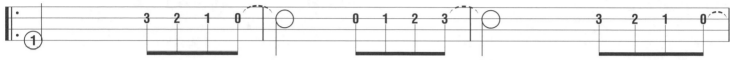

Verse

1. Like a fool I went and stayed too long. Now I'm wonderin' if your love's
2. Then that time I went and said goodbye. Now I'm back and not ashamed

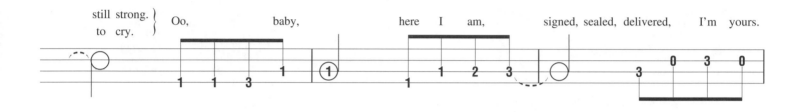

still strong. Oo, baby, here I am, signed, sealed, delivered, I'm yours.
to cry.

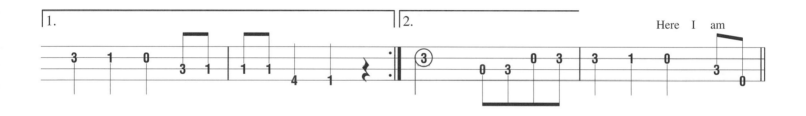

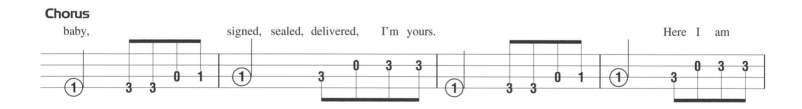

Chorus

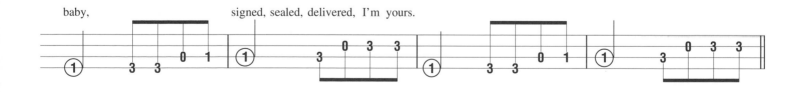

Outro

Words and Music by Stevie Wonder, Syreeta Wright, Lee Garrett and Lula Mae Hardaway
© 1970 (Renewed 1998) JOBETE MUSIC CO., INC., BLACK BULL MUSIC and SAWANDI MUSIC
c/o EMI APRIL MUSIC INC. and EMI BLACKWOOD MUSIC INC.

PLAYING WITH A PICK

A pick produces a clear, distinct sound, and is a popular choice for rock bass. Some of rock's greatest bassists like Paul McCartney (The Beatles), Chris Squire (Yes), and Krist Novoselic (Nirvana) use a pick almost exclusively, while many others switch between pick and fingerstyle.

Picks come in various thicknesses. For the bass, a medium to heavy gauge pick will give you the best tone. To hold it properly, first curl your index finger and place the pick on top with the tip sticking out. Then place your thumb over the top of the pick and hold it firmly. There should be about 3/8 inch of the tip extending out. Place the flat side of the pick against the string, and drag the pick across.

You can pick with either downstrokes (⊓) or upstrokes (∨). Downstrokes produce a stronger sound, but upstrokes are used in conjunction with downstrokes when playing faster bass lines, or when the specific sound of alternating strokes is required for a song.

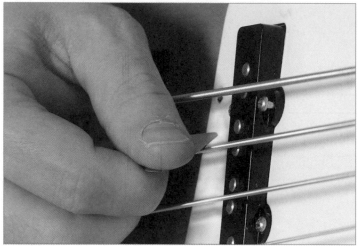

Downstroke

Upstroke

ADAM'S SONG

Try picking with all downstrokes on this Blink-182 bass line the first few times. Afterwards, play it again with alternating strokes (down-up-down-up) to feel and hear the difference.

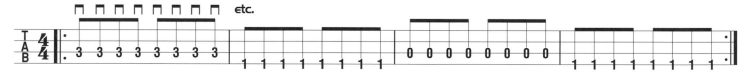

VERTIGO

This U2 song has a bass part that's a little tricky. Always begin slowly when playing a new song and gradually work it up to speed.

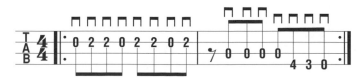

COME AS YOU ARE

The last two song examples were driving, rock bass lines that sound good picked with all downstrokes. This riff by Nirvana, by contrast, requires a looser feel that can be achieved with alternate picking. As a general rule, upstrokes are used on the "and" of beats as noted here.

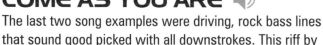

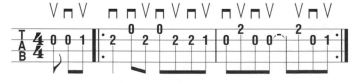

ROXANNE

Sting, the bassist and singer of the band the Police, used a pick on the song "Roxanne." You can play the bass lines to the intro, verse, and pre-chorus with all downstrokes to get a strong, even sound. Then switch to alternate picking for the eighth notes leading into the chorus.

Once you reach the end of the interlude section on the second page, you'll see the instructions "D.S. al Coda." Jump back to the sign (𝄋) at the beginning of the verse and play up to the instruction "To Coda." At this point, skip to the last line of the tune that is labeled "Coda," and play the final four measures.

Intro

1. Rox -

The sign

𝄋 **Verse**

anne,   you don't have to   put on the red light.
loved you since I knew ya,   I wouldn't talk down to ya.   I

Those days are over,   you don't have to   sell   your body   to the night.   Rox -
have to   tell you just how I feel,   I won't   share   you with another   boy.   I

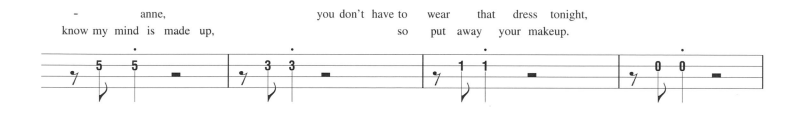

-       anne,   you don't have to   wear   that   dress tonight,
know my mind is made up,   so   put   away   your makeup.

walk   the streets   for money,   you don't care   if   it's wrong or if it's right. ⎫   Rox -
Told   you once, I   won't tell you again.   It's   a   bad   way.   ⎭

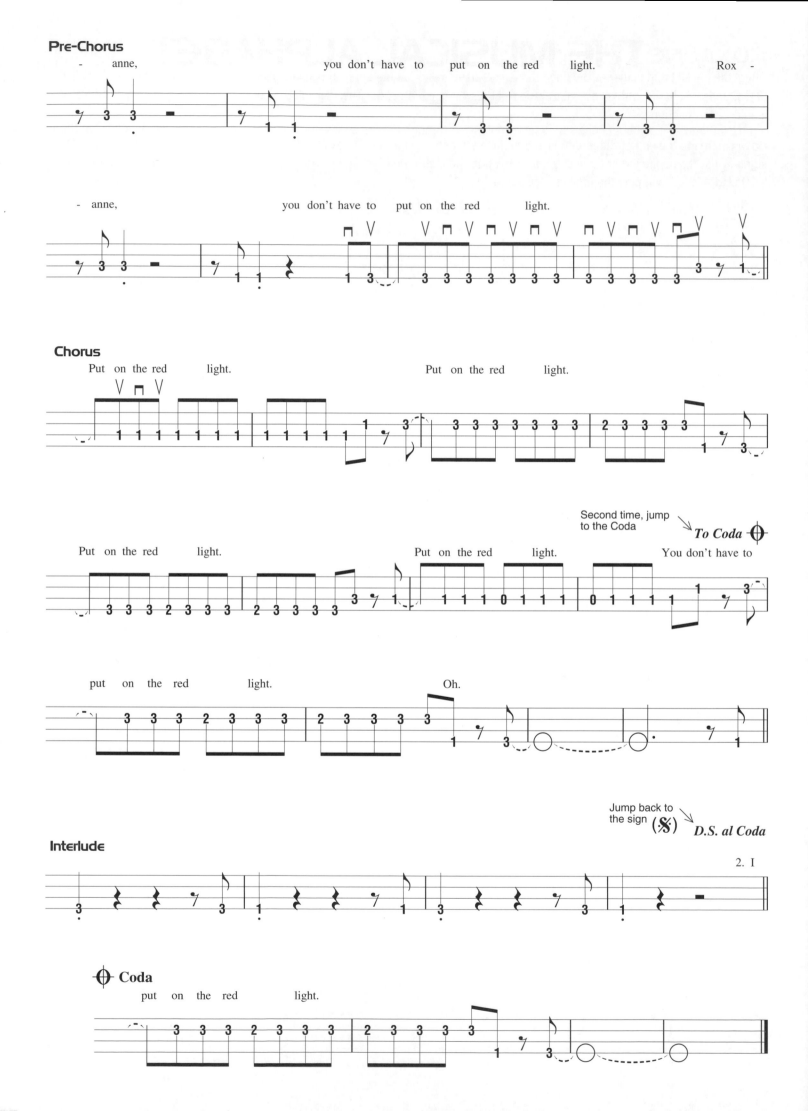

THE MUSICAL ALPHABET AND OCTAVES

The basic musical alphabet consists of seven notes—A through G. This series of notes repeats as you extend beyond G at the top or descend beyond A below.

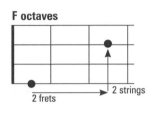

The distance from any one note to the same note up or down eight letters in the musical alphabet is called an **octave**. The two notes of the octave will share the same letter name and sound very much alike, except one will be higher and the other lower in pitch.

Octaves follow a movable pattern on the fretboard. To find an octave above any note on the E or A string, move up two frets and across two strings as illustrated below.

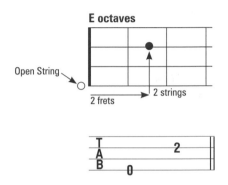

LOVE ROLLERCOASTER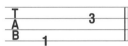

This song was a #1 hit for funk group the Ohio Players and was later covered by the Red Hot Chili Peppers. Follow the indicated fret-hand fingerings and alternate your picking fingers. Pluck the lower notes with your index finger and the higher octave notes with your middle finger.

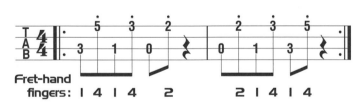

Words and Music by Ralph Middlebrooks, James Williams, Marshall Jones, Leroy Bonner,
Clarence Satchell, William Beck and Marvin Pierce
© 1975 (Renewed 2003) SEGUNDO SUENOS (BMI)/Administered by BUG MUSIC, INC., A BMG CHRYSALIS
COMPANY and RICK'S MUSIC INC. (BMI)/Administered by RIGHTSONG MUSIC INC.

MY SHARONA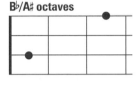

On the repeat of this riff by the Knack, fret the low F# with your 1st finger. Then shift your hand up one fret to begin again at G with the same finger.

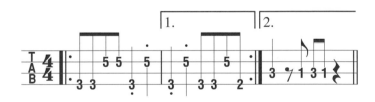

Words and Music by Doug Fieger and Berton Averre
Copyright © 1979 by Three Wise Boys Music, LLC (BMI), Small Hill Music (ASCAP) and Eighties Music (ASCAP)
All Rights for Small Hill Music and Eighties Music Controlled and Administered by Hi Pitch Music Services

SMOKE ON THE WATER

The verse section of this legendary rock song consists of mostly G and F octave notes.

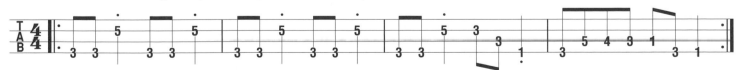

Words and Music by Ritchie Blackmore, Ian Gillan, Roger Glover, Jon Lord and Ian Paice
© 1972 (Renewed 2000) B. FELDMAN & CO. LTD. trading as HEC MUSIC
All Rights for the United States and Canada Controlled and Administered by GLENWOOD MUSIC CORP.

THE BOX SHAPE

The **box shape** is a four-note, moveable pattern on the fretboard that can be found in bass lines of all styles. The lowest note in the pattern is called the **root note**, and the highest is the octave. The root note got its name because it serves as the strongest note of the group from which everything else is based.

Below are illustrations of the box shape on the fretboard in a few different positions.

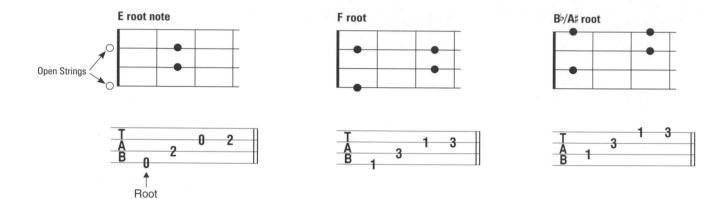

PUNCHING BAG

This bass line starts on the root note A and is a great practice for the rake technique if using your fingers.

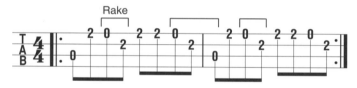

NIGHT TRAIN

Follow the correct fret-hand fingering on this James Brown bass riff to minimize hand stress.

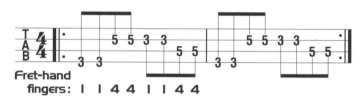

WHAT'D I SAY

The box shape can often be found in blues songs like this classic by Ray Charles. "What'd I Say" is an example of a twelve-measure, repeating song form called a **12-bar blues**.

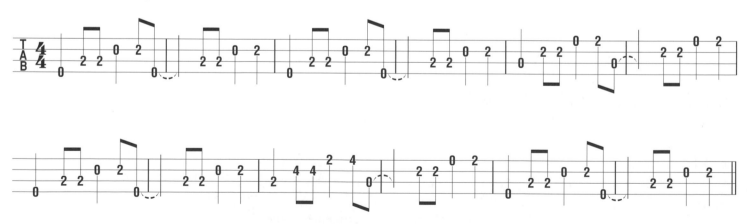

BLACK MAGIC WOMAN

The box shape can be played anywhere on the neck of the bass. For this song made famous by Santana, we're moving a little beyond the notes we have learned so far to illustrate this idea.

In any song, the bass line corresponds directly to **chords** that a guitarist or pianist plays. These chords are notated with **chord symbols** found above the staff. Notice that the root note of the box shape moves along with the changing chords.

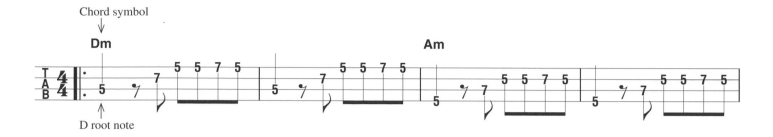

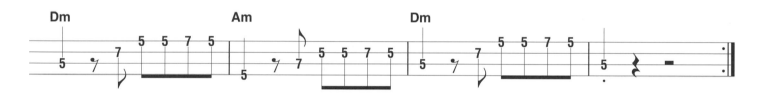

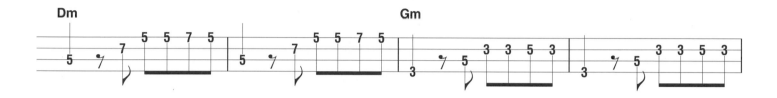

JUMPIN' AND JIVIN'

Here is one more example of a 12-bar blues. This one goes beyond the box shape by adding some outside notes to the mix, but it's a must-know, standard bass line that has been used in countless jazz, blues, and rockabilly songs.

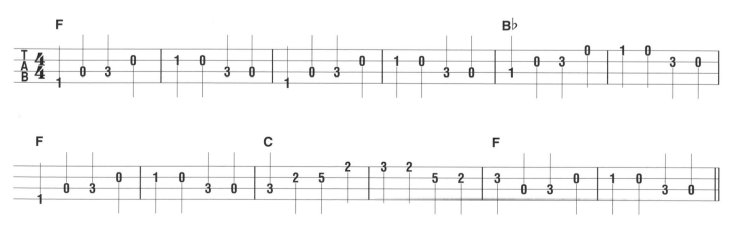

MORE RHYTHMS

You've already learned that a dot after a note increases the value by one half. Therefore a **dotted quarter note** lasts for 1-1/2 beats.

A very common bass rhythm that incorporates the dotted quarter note is shown below. For counting, it can be helpful to think of a dotted quarter note as a quarter tied to an eighth.

RIKKI DON'T LOSE THAT NUMBER

A latin-inspired bass line serves as an introduction to this Steely Dan song.

Count: one (two) and three (four) and

DEVILS HAIRCUT

This song by Beck can be played with a finger roll across all three strings.

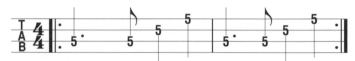

Count: one (two) and three four

WEREWOLVES OF LONDON

The rhythm from the last two examples is reversed here.

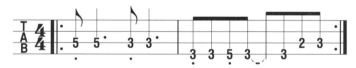

THE END

As made famous by Duke Ellington, this short riff is a standard ending to a lot of songs.

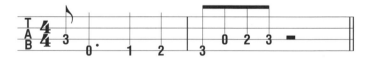

FEEL GOOD INC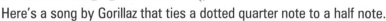

Here's a song by Gorillaz that ties a dotted quarter note to a half note.

OH, PRETTY WOMAN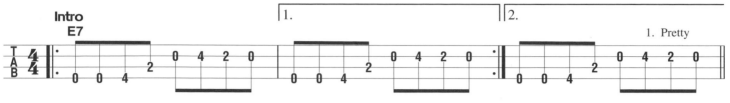

Sometimes the time signature, or **meter**, can change within a song as it does in this one by Roy Orbison. A measure of 2/4 time has two beats, and a quarter note receives one beat. The meter changes in this song happen for only one measure before changing back to 4/4, so count aloud to help get through those passages.

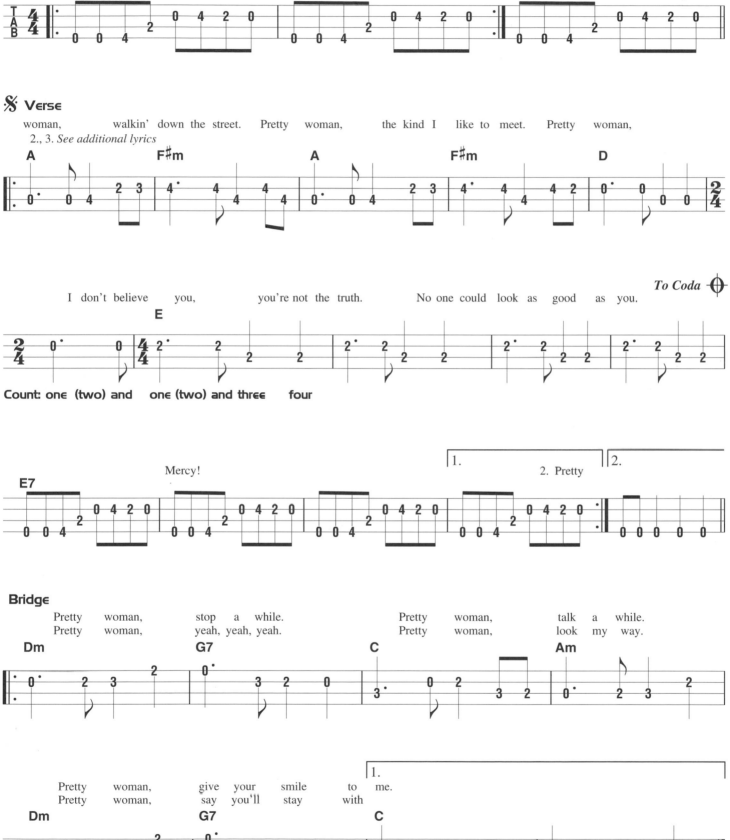

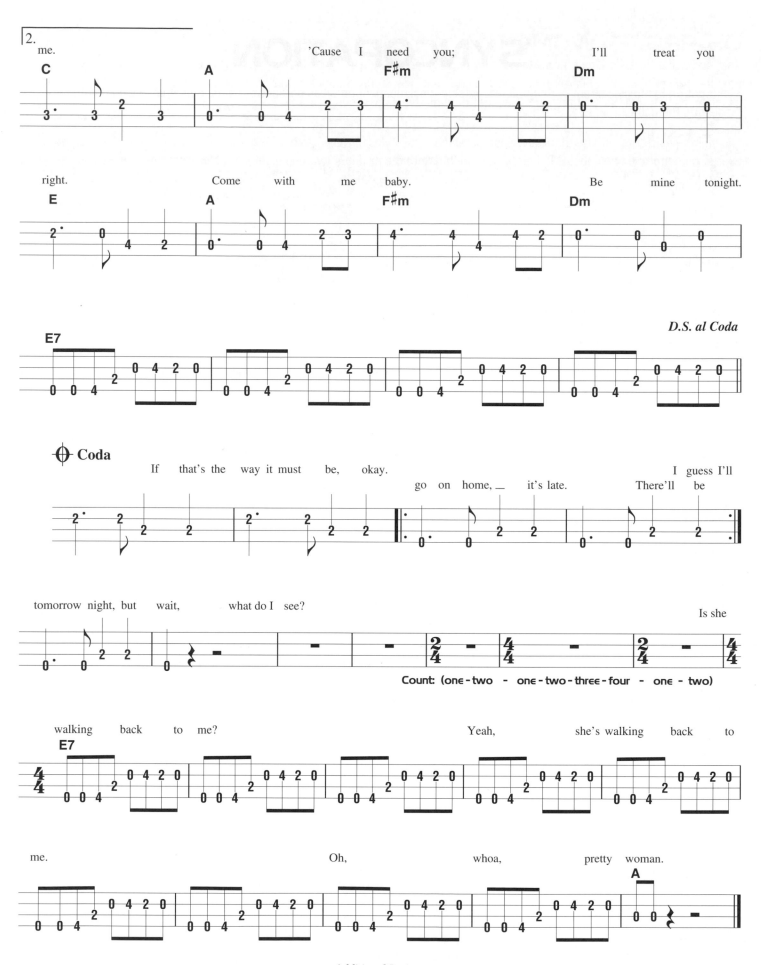

Additional Lyrics

2. Pretty woman, won't you pardon me?
   Pretty woman, I couldn't help but see;
   Pretty woman, that you look lovely as can be.
   Are you lonely just like me?

3. Pretty woman, don't walk on by.
   Pretty woman, don't make me cry.
   Pretty woman, don't walk away.
   Okay.

SYNCOPATION

Syncopation is the placement of rhythmic accents on weak beats or on weak portions of beats. Syncopated eighth notes emphasize the upbeat, or "and" of a beat.

The eighth–quarter–eighth rhythm shown here is found in all styles of music. What makes this rhythm a little tricky is that the quarter note starts on an upbeat. To help, count the quarter note as if it is two tied eighth notes as illustrated below.

RADAR LOVE

This driving rock song by Golden Earring features a picked bass intro, but it can also be played fingerstyle.

GREEN ACRES THEME

The classic TV show "Green Acres" used this tune as a theme.

PROUD MARY

In the first and second measures of this song recorded by Creedence Clearwater Revival, there are accents on the "and" of beat 2. The third measure, however, contains the most syncopated part of the whole intro with accents on the "and" of beats 2, 3, and 4.

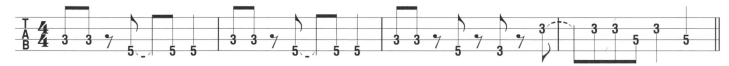

MUSTANG SALLY

Many artists have recorded this song through the years, but Wilson Pickett's version has become a timeless soul classic.
The syncopated bass line supplies a bouncy feel that is the foundation for what the other instruments play.

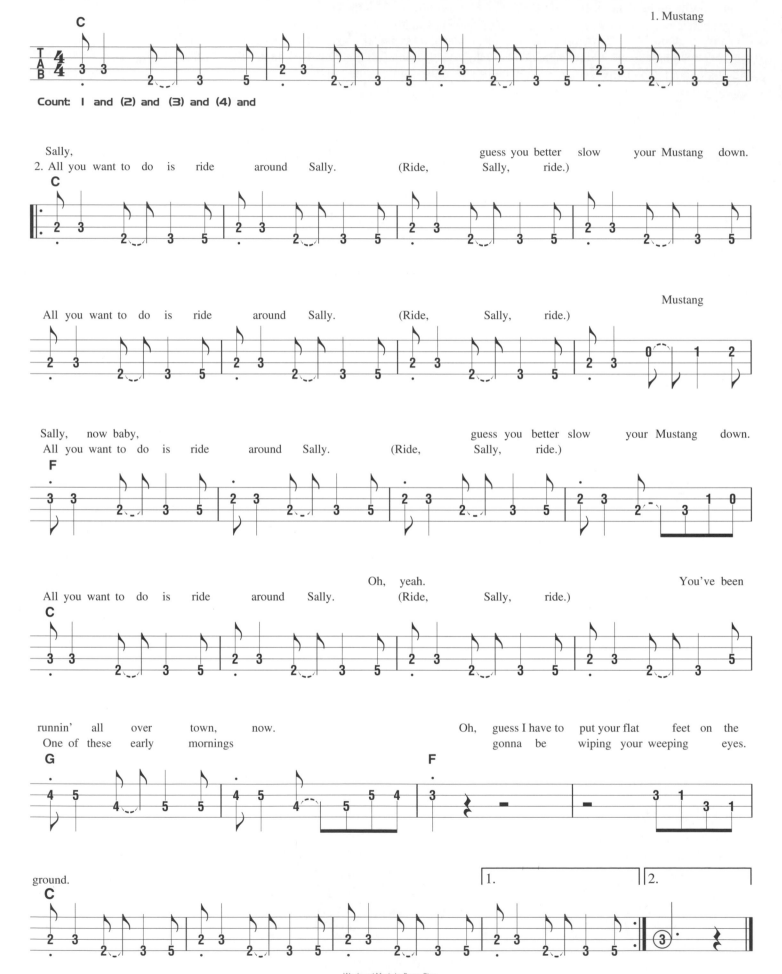

SLIDES, HAMMER-ONS & PULL-OFFS

Sometimes, it's not so much what you play, it's how you play it. In music terms, this is called **articulation**. Slides, hammer-ons, and pull-offs all belong to a special category of articulations called **legato**. Legato techniques allow you to connect two or more consecutive notes together to create a smooth, flowing sound.

To play a **slide**, pick the first note as you normally would. Then, maintain pressure as you move your fret-hand finger up or down the fretboard to sound the second note. (The second note is not picked.) In tab, a slide is indicated with a short, slanted line and a curved **slur**.

SWEET LEAF

Here is a classic heavy metal riff by the band Black Sabbath. Execute the first slide from D to D♭ with your 2nd finger. That will set you up to play C with your 1st finger.

Words and Music by Frank Iommi, John Osbourne, William Ward and Terence Butler
© Copyright 1971 (Renewed) and 1974 (Renewed) Westminster Music Ltd., London, England
TRO - Essex Music International, Inc., New York, controls all publication rights for the U.S.A. and Canada

THE BEETLE

If this bass line sounds familiar, it's because there are many recorded variations of it throughout popular music. Use your 4th finger to execute both slides in this example.

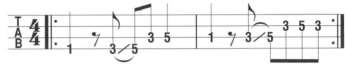

Copyright © 2013 by HAL LEONARD CORPORATION

THE MUNSTERS THEME

Beginning in measure 3, slide from F to F♯ with your 3rd finger and play the top note (B on the G string) with your 4th in this TV theme song.

By Jack Marshall
Copyright © 1973 SONGS OF UNIVERSAL, INC.
Copyright Renewed

To play a **hammer-on**, pluck the first note and then press down, or "hammer on" to, a higher note along the same string. The initial attack should carry over to produce sound from the second note without picking again. If the first note is fretted, it helps to keep the first note held down when executing the hammer-on.

In tab, a hammer-on is notated with a curved slur connecting two notes.

MOUNTAIN SONG
This Jane's Addiction song features a cool bass line with a couple hammer-ons on the D string.

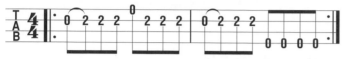

TAXATION
Here's an ode to a famous bass line that uses the box shape.

BRING IT ON HOME
The **grace-note slide** on the "and" of beat 4 in this Led Zeppelin riff denotes a very quick slide to the primary (second) note.

LOW RIDER
The bass riff to "Low Rider" may be one of the most recognizable in rock music. Keep your 1st finger planted through both hammer-ons.

Fret-hand fingers: 1 4   1   4 4   1   4 1 4 1 4

A **pull-off** is the opposite of a hammer-on. It is the technique used to slur from a higher note to a lower one. Start with your finger planted on the first note of the slur. Pluck the higher note and then tug, or "pull," that finger off the string to sound the lower note.

LEAD BALLOON
It's a common mistake when attempting a pull-off to pull the string out of tune before the release. This is usually the result of simply pulling too hard.

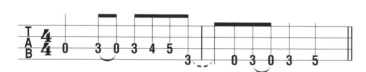

CULT OF PERSONALITY
Start with your 2nd finger on G and use your 3rd finger to execute the pull-off for this riff by Living Colour.

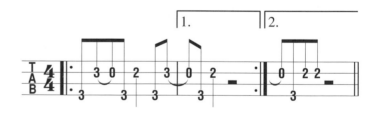

LOVE IN AN ELEVATOR
This is the intro riff to one of Aerosmith's biggest hits. The fingering below will help set you up for the pull-off on the A string.

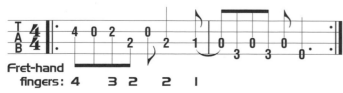

Fret-hand fingers: 4   3 2   2   1

RAIN
You can combine legato articulations as this Beatles bass line demonstrates. The last three notes in measure 2 meld a hammer-on and pull-off in one continuous motion. Keep your 1st finger planted on the F through the entire hammer-on/pull-off combination.

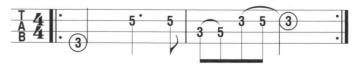

OTHERSIDE

What better way to wrap up this book than with one of the Red Hot Chili Peppers' biggest hits. The bass line to "Otherside" contains slides, hammer-ons, syncopated rhythms, and more!

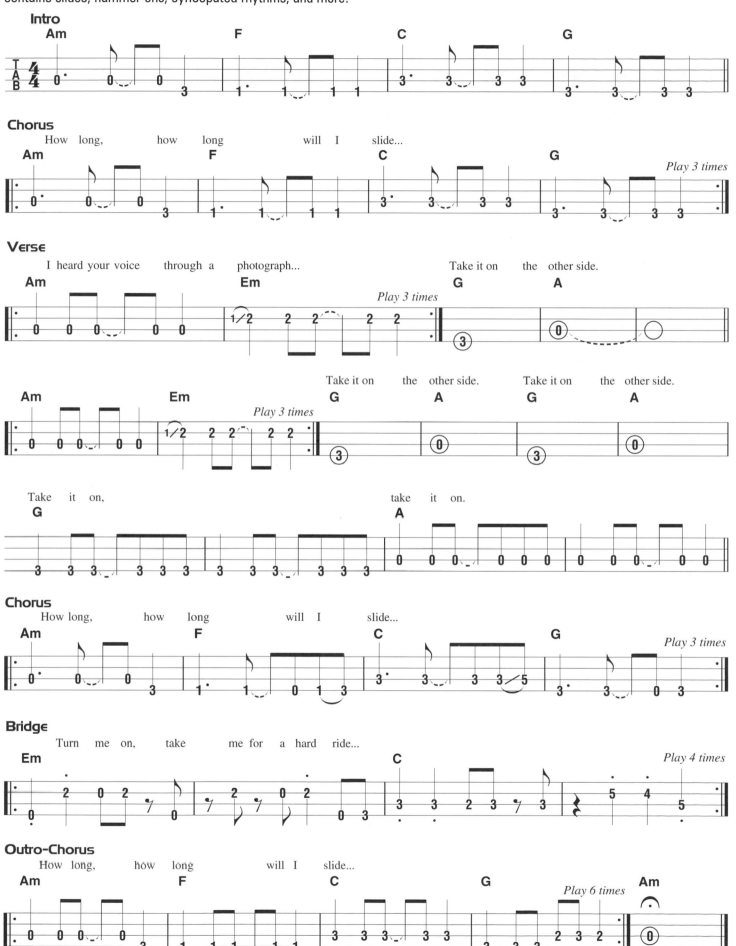

Words and Music by Anthony Kiedis, Flea, John Frusciante and Chad Smith
© 1999 MOEBETOBLAME MUSIC

MOVIN' UP THE FRETBOARD

Earlier we learned all of the notes within the first five frets. Now let's move beyond the first five frets and start playing "up the neck." Here are the notes within frets 5–12 on the two lowest strings.

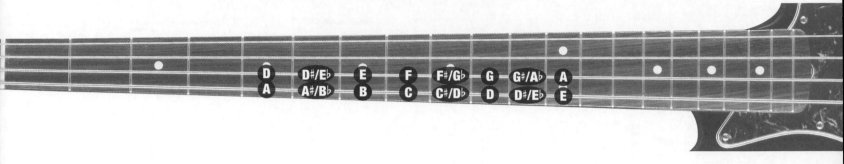

The following song examples utilize the notes on the E and A strings above the 5th fret. After becoming comfortable playing each riff, try naming the notes aloud.

GET READY

This song, originally written for the Temptations by Smokey Robinson, became a hit for the rock band Rare Earth in 1970. The riff is played up the neck at the 8th and 10th frets of the E and A strings. Starting with your third finger on the 10th fret will put your hand in the right position.

MY GIRL

Try this Motown classic by the Temptations. It's a perfect place to practice the rake technique from Book One. Remember? (i) = index and (m) = middle.

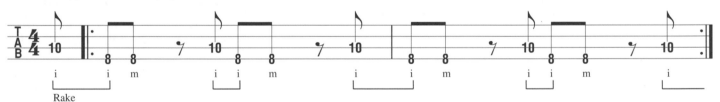

GOOD PEOPLE

Here's a bass line from Jack Johnson that jumps from the 7th fret up to the 11th fret. Try the fingering pattern written below for minimal hand movement.

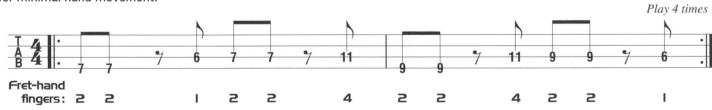

ONE LOVE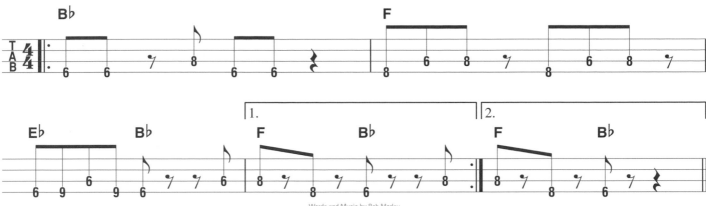

One advantage of playing on the lower two strings is that they have a bigger, beefier sound. In general, the larger the string, the deeper the tone produced. This song by Bob Marley and the Wailers could be played in first position, but then it wouldn't have the deep bass sound that is signature to the reggae style.

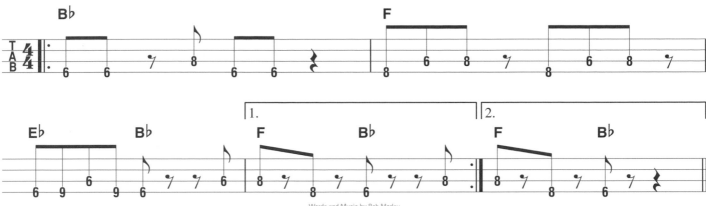

JAMMING

In this Bob Marley classic, bassist Aston "Family Man" Barrett lays down another great bass line using the low strings. This one can be played using one finger per fret, meaning each finger is assigned a fret. The 7th fret is played with the first finger, the 10th with the fourth finger, and the 9th is played with the third.

D STRING, FRETS 5-12

Let's add the D string in the mix. Here are the notes within frets 5–12 on the D string.

MICHELLE

Here we introduce the C and B-flat on the D string in this ballad by the Beatles.

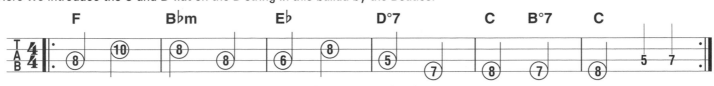

BEAST OF BURDEN

Here's a classic by the Rolling Stones that introduces the A and B notes on the D string. Remember from Book One that a staccato mark means hold the note shorter than its normal value.

Words and Music by Mick Jagger and Keith Richards
© 1978 EMI MUSIC PUBLISHING LTD.
All Rights for the U.S. and Canada Controlled and Administered by COLGEMS-EMI MUSIC INC.
All Rights Reserved   International Copyright Secured   Used by Permission

I WISH

In this hit song by Stevie Wonder we'll tune down the open strings a **half step** (one fret). Some artists/bands tune down their instruments to accommodate a singer's vocal range or to sound heavier. In this case the E becomes Eb, A = Ab, D = Db, and G = Gb.

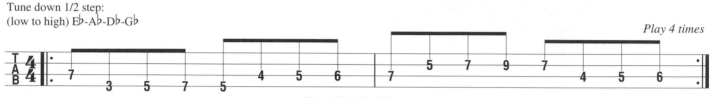

Words and Music by Stevie Wonder
© 1976 (Renewed 2004) JOBETE MUSIC CO., INC. and BLACK BULL MUSIC
c/o EMI APRIL MUSIC INC.
All Rights Reserved   International Copyright Secured   Used by Permission

HOLIDAY IN CAMBODIA

This bass riff by the American hardcore punk band Dead Kennedys requires you to play two notes simultaneously, a technique called a **double stop**. Using a pick, strum with downstrokes across both strings so they ring out evenly in volume.

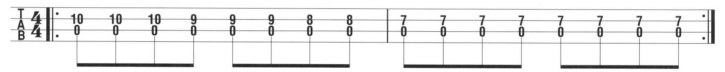

Words and Music by Bruce Slesinger, Darren Henley, Raymond Pepperelle, Geoffrey Lyall and Eric Boucher
Copyright © 1980 Decay Music
All Rights Administered by Songs Of Kobalt Music Publishing
All Rights Reserved   Used by Permission

DRIVEN TO TEARS

For this Police song use the **box shape** that you learned in Book One starting at the 5th fret.

Music and Lyrics by Sting
© 1980 G.M. SUMNER
Administered by EMI MUSIC PUBLISHING LIMITED
All Rights Reserved   International Copyright Secured   Used by Permission

NOWHERE MAN

Here's another Beatles song from their album *Rubber Soul*. This one will be a challenge because of the syncopated rhythms at this faster tempo. Learn the bass part without the backing track at first, and once you know it well, try playing along. Begin each verse section with your 2nd finger on the 7th fret and stay in that position using one finger per fret.

Verse

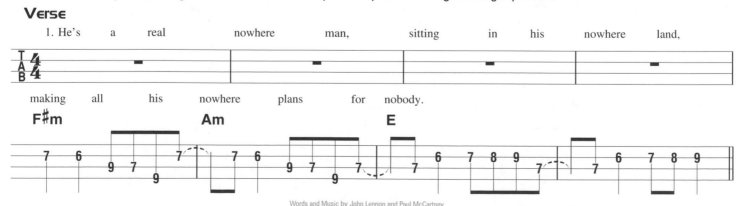

Words and Music by John Lennon and Paul McCartney
Copyright © 1965 Sony/ATV Music Publishing LLC
Copyright Renewed
All Rights Administered by Sony/ATV Music Publishing LLC, 424 Church Street, Suite 1200, Nashville, TN 37219
International Copyright Secured   All Rights Reserved

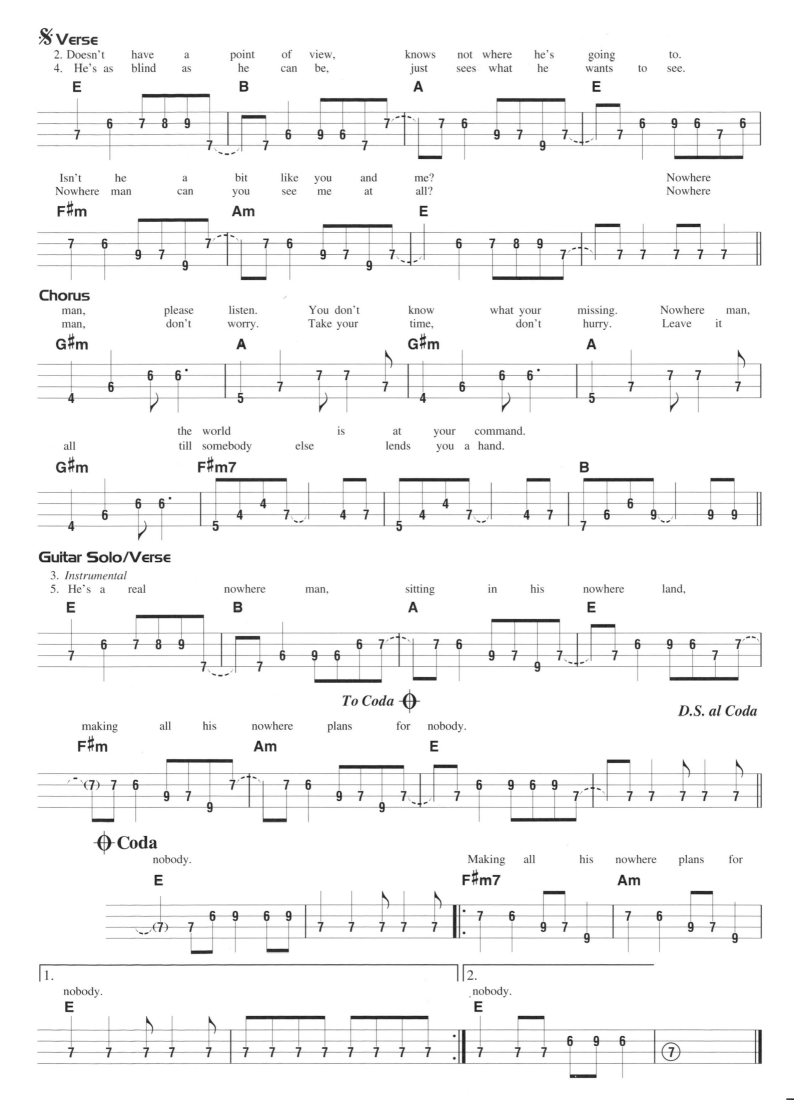

G STRING, FRETS 5-12

Here are the notes within frets 5–12 on the G string.

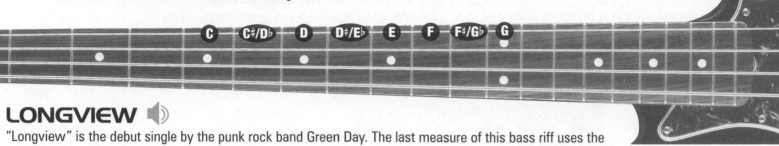

LONGVIEW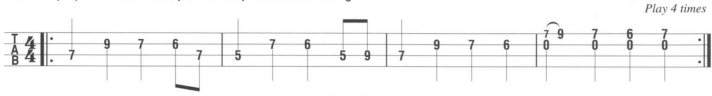

"Longview" is the debut single by the punk rock band Green Day. The last measure of this bass riff uses the
G string, a hammer-on, and a double stop. Green Day tuned their guitars and bass down a half step to record the song,
but for the purpose of this book, you can stay in standard tuning.

Play 4 times

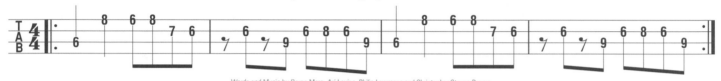

RUNAWAY BABY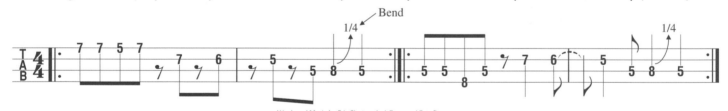

Here we introduce the D-flat and E-flat on the G string in this song by Bruno Mars.

SUNSHINE OF YOUR LOVE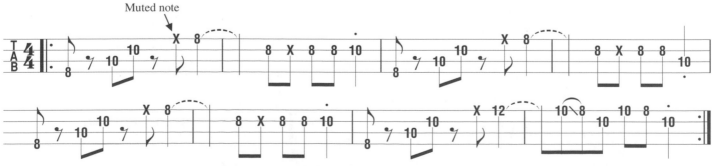

This song by the British rock band Cream uses a technique called a **bend**. String bending allows us to emulate the scooped notes of
the human voice. The fret-hand fingers push or pull the string out of its normal alignment, stretching it so the pitch of the note is raised.
For this song we will use a quarter-step bend which raises the pitch halfway between the note plucked and a half step (one fret).

PERCUSSIVE

In this funky bass line you will notice an X in the tab staff instead of a number. An X represents a **muted note**. Muted notes
(sometimes called dead notes) produce a percussive sound without an actual pitch that can be used to enhance the rhythmic feel
of a bass line. For the example below, lightly lift your fret-hand finger off of the fretboard while still touching the string. Then strike
the string with your picking hand to produce the muted sound.

DAY TRIPPER

You might remember this song from earlier in the book. We simplified the bass riff at that time to help teach technique and reading, but the bass line here is the real deal. This is what Paul McCartney played on the Beatles recording.

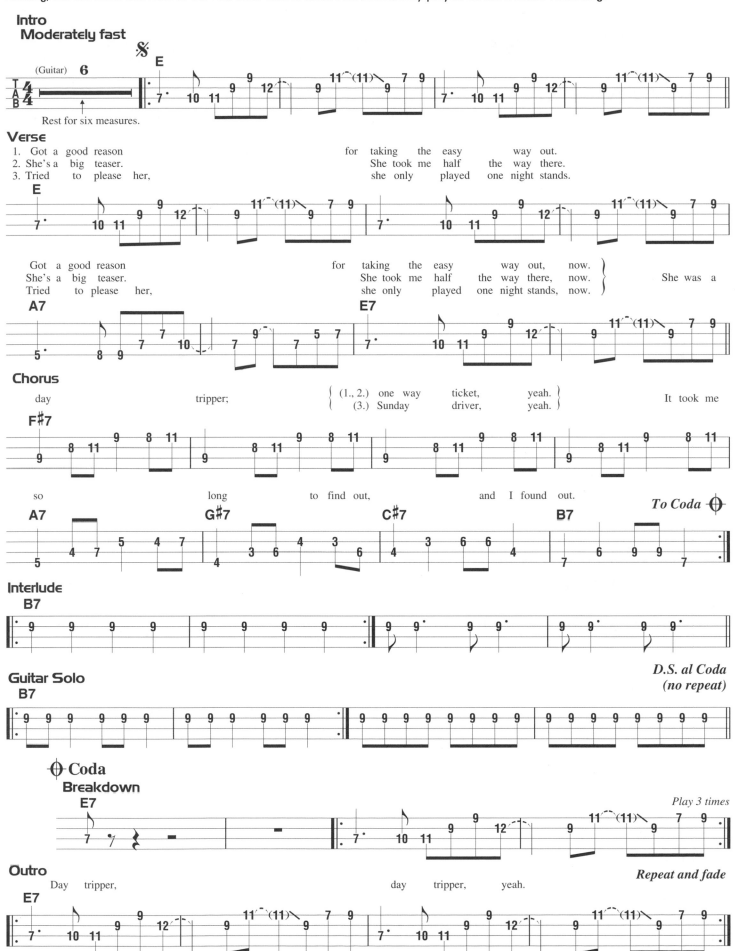

NEW RHYTHMS

A **sixteenth note** lasts half as long as an eighth note, and is written with two flags or two beams. There are four sixteenth notes in one beat.

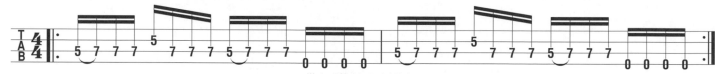

MOUNTAIN SONG

The main riff in this song by Jane's Addiction uses a repetitive pattern of sixteenth notes. Divide each beat into four parts, and count "one-e-and-a, two-e-and-a, three-e-and-a, four-e-and-a."

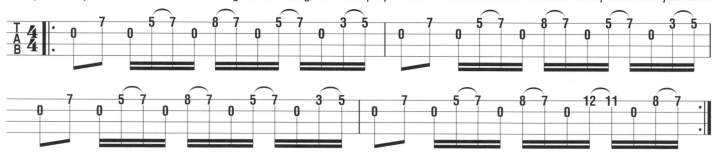

FORTY SIX & 2

Here's a fun intro bass riff by the band Tool. Be sure that all sixteenth notes are played evenly—the hammer-ons and pull-offs can throw you off if you're not careful. On the original recording, the bass player used a chorus effect to achieve the special tone you hear.

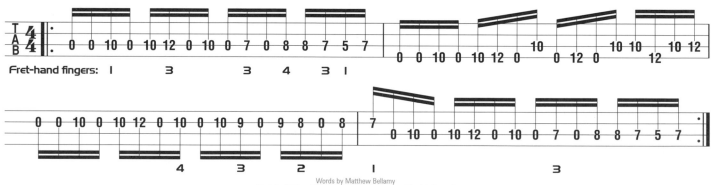

HYSTERIA

Ready to speed it up? With a pick, use steady, alternating downstrokes and upstrokes for the sixteenth notes in this song by the alternative rock band Muse. The movement of the notes can be tricky for your fretting hand, so there are a few fingering suggestions below the staff to help out.

UNDER PRESSURE

This highly recognizable song was from a collaboration between the band Queen and David Bowie. The second beat mixes an eighth note and two sixteenths.

WOULD?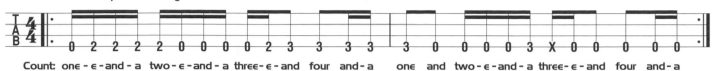

One of the most popular songs by the band Alice in Chains combines eighth and sixteenth note variations on beats three and four. Count this one slowly at first to get the feel.

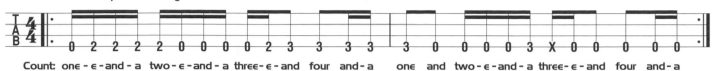

THE TROOPER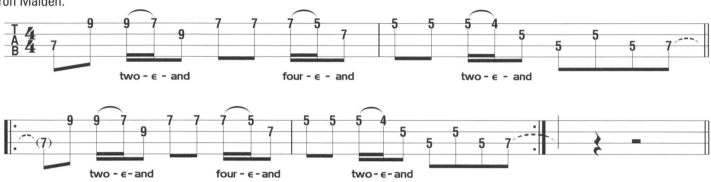

Let's continue on a theme with another great bass intro combining sixteenth and eighth notes, written by Steve Harris of the band Iron Maiden.

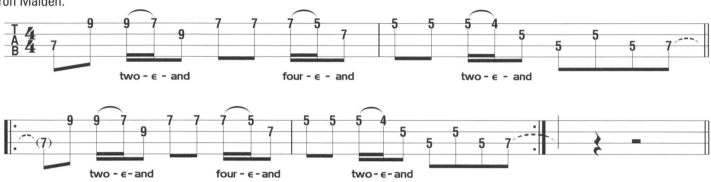

NO MORE TEARS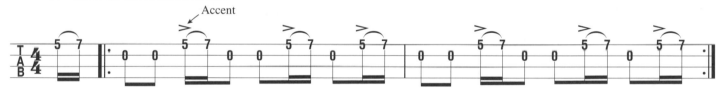

Clocking in at over seven minutes, this is the longest song recorded by British heavy metal vocalist Ozzy Osbourne. It starts with a double sixteenth-note pickup and introduces an **accent** (>), which tells the player to strike a note louder or with a harder attack than the surrounding, unaccented notes.

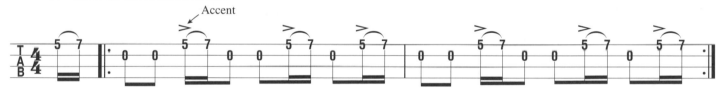

ACE OF SPADES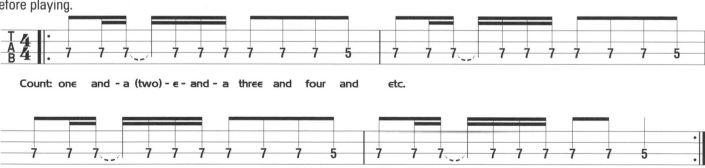

There's a sixteenth note tie in this classic metal anthem by Mötorhead. Go slow and count it through until the rhythm is familiar before playing.

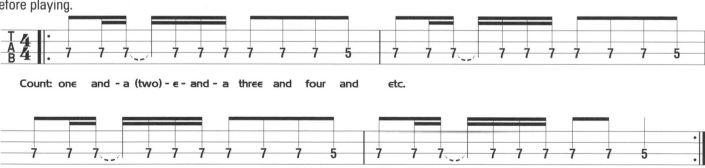

GREEN STEW

This rock riff mixes groups of sixteenth notes with eighth rests. Descending bass lines similar to this one have been used in many songs like "25 or 6 to 4" by Chicago, "Brain Stew" by Green Day, and the end of "Stairway to Heaven" by Led Zeppelin.

A **sixteenth rest** takes up the same time as a sixteenth note, a quarter of a beat. It looks like this:

$$\overset{\scriptstyle 4}{7} = 1/4 \text{ beat} \qquad \overset{\scriptstyle 4}{7} + \overset{\scriptstyle 4}{7} = \overset{\scriptstyle 4}{7}$$

SIXTEEN

To get started playing with sixteenth rests, try this rock groove at a slow tempo and count.

Count: one - ϵ -(and)-a   two- ϵ -(and)-a   three- ϵ -(and)-a   four- ϵ - and - a

FLY AWAY

This song was a hit for Lenny Kravitz in 1998. The part written here is the intro, and the funky, slap bass groove of the verses is taught later in this book.

EXODUS

Here's a Bob Marley song for sixteenth note and rest practice.

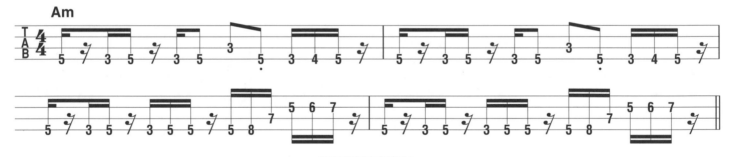

Another common rest pattern you'll notice when working with sixteenth notes is the **dotted eighth rest**. You've already learned that a dot after a note or rest increases the value by one half. Therefore, a dotted eighth rest lasts for 3/4 of a beat.

$$\overset{\scriptstyle}{7} + \overset{\scriptstyle 4}{7} = \overset{\scriptstyle}{7}{\cdot} \qquad \text{or} \qquad \overset{\scriptstyle 4}{7} + \overset{\scriptstyle 4}{7} + \overset{\scriptstyle 4}{7} = \overset{\scriptstyle}{7}{\cdot}$$

SELF ESTEEM

This is a song by the American punk rock group the Offspring. On beat two, the dotted eighth rest takes up the last 3/4 of the beat and on beat three it takes up the first 3/4 of the beat.

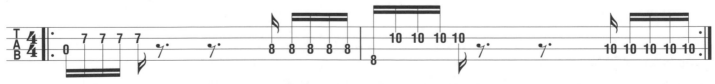

Count: one- ϵ -and-a   two-(ϵ-and-a) (three- ϵ -and)-a   four- ϵ -and-a   one- ϵ - and - a   two-(ϵ - and - a) (three- ϵ - and) - a   four- ϵ - and - a

PLUSH

The Stone Temple Pilots recorded this song on their 1992 debut studio album *Core*.

Here's another common rhythm to learn and memorize—a dotted eighth and sixteenth note over one beat. It has two forms: a dotted eighth note followed by a sixteenth, and the reverse, a sixteenth note followed by a dotted eighth.

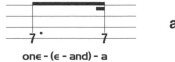 and

TWO WAYS OF ONE

First, try playing these rhythms with just one note to get the feel and to practice counting.

DANI CALIFORNIA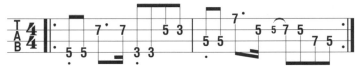

Here's an example of this new rhythm in a Red Hot Chili Peppers song. Also, notice the box shape (taught in Book One) within this bass line as it moves through the chord progression.

PEACE SELLS

The music video for this Megadeth song became an MTV regular and the opening bass riff was used as the MTV News intro. More recently, VH1 ranked "Peace Sells" at number 11 on their list of the "40 Greatest Metal Songs of All Time."

Play 4 times

SWEET EMOTION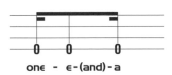

With this rockin' riff by Aerosmith, we introduce one more sixteenth/eighth note variation: a sixteenth–eighth–sixteenth pattern. Practice the new rhythm with just one note on the bass before attempting the song.

HARD TO HANDLE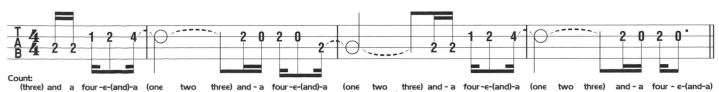

Otis Redding wrote and recorded this song in 1968, and it later became the breakout single for the Black Crowes in 1990. Count aloud as you play through.

Count:
(three) and a four-ϵ-(and)-a (one   two   three) and - a four-ϵ-(and)-a (one   two   three) and - a four-ϵ-(and)-a

BRICK HOUSE 🔊

The various rhythms in this Commodores funk classic are a little tricky. Try learning each measure separately before attempting to play the whole bass line.

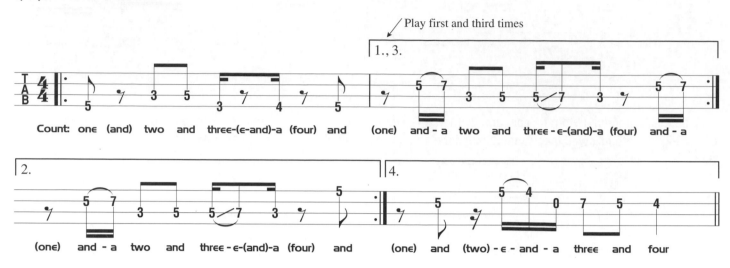

AMERICAN WOMAN 🔊

Now let's mix up the past few rhythms we've covered in this song by the Guess Who.

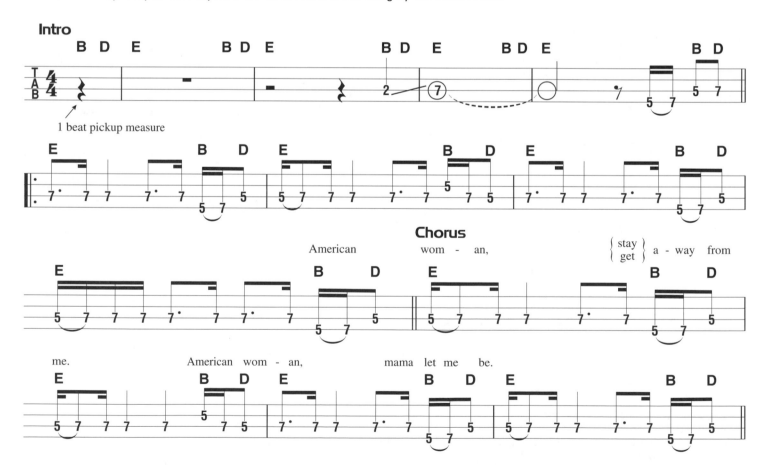

Verse

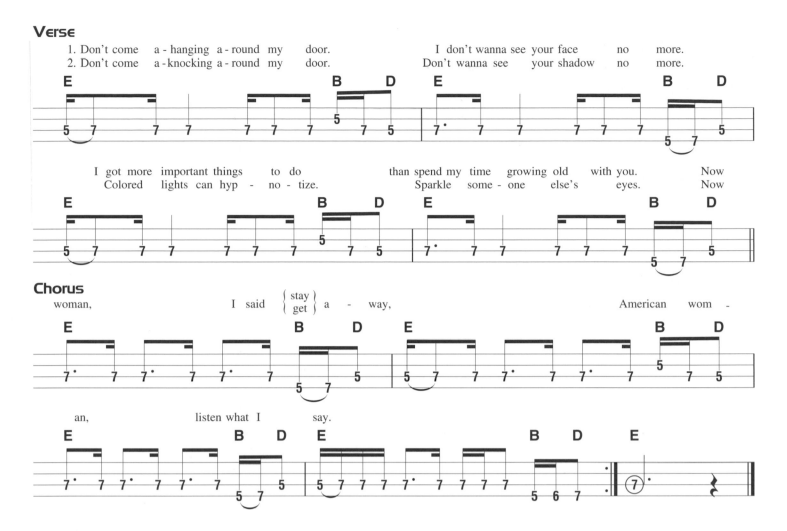

Chorus

SHAKE YOUR BODY DOWN TO THE GROUND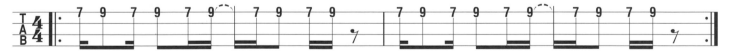

Counting becomes more of a challenge when adding ties to sixteenth notes, as is demonstrated with this Michael Jackson bass line.

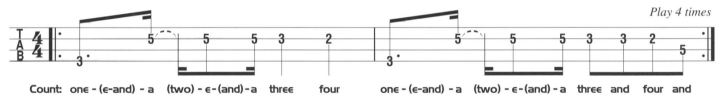

CAN'T STOP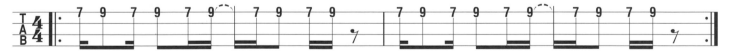

Here's the guitar intro to the Red Hot Chili Pepper's song "Can't Stop."

ROOT DOWN

This funky, syncopated bass line was sampled by the Beastie Boys from a Jimmy Smith album and used as the main groove to their song "Root Down."

A **triplet** is a group of three notes played in the space of two. Whereas eighth notes divide a beat into two parts, **eighth-note triplets** divide a beat into three parts.

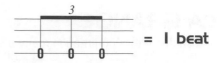

ADDAMS FAMILY THEME

While playing the riff from this classic TV series, count the new rhythm by simply saying the word "tri-pl-et."

Count: tri - pl - et   one (two three)   tri - pl - et   one   etc.

GET UP STAND UP

Here's another well-known Bob Marley song for triplet practice. Listen to the recorded example to hear what eighth-note triplets sound like at this slower tempo.

LONDON CALLING

Use your 1st finger to slide up to the 7th fret (E) from the 2nd (B). This will set up your hand in the correct position to reach the remaining notes. In the last measure, hold the C at the 8th fret for two beats before sliding down on beat 3.

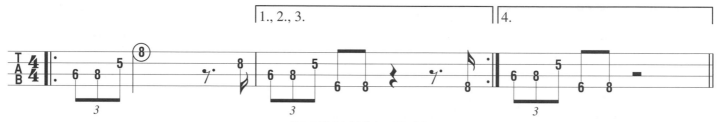

I'M YOUR HOOCHIE COOCHIE MAN

This is a blues standard written by Willie Dixon and first recorded by Muddy Waters in 1954. Count the beginning triplet figure with two rests the same way you've counted the previous triplets. A bracket above the notes takes the place of a beam to label the triplet grouping with rests.

Count: (tri - pl) - let   tri - pl - et

A **shuffle** is a bouncy, skipping, rhythmic feel. Eighth notes are played as long-short, rather than as equal values. This feel is the same as inserting a rest in the middle of a triplet or tying the first two eighth notes of a triplet.

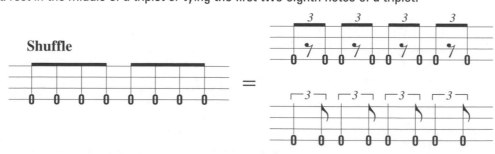

LA GRANGE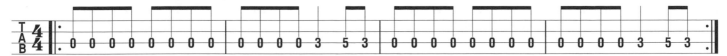

The shuffle feel is common in many blues and blues-rock songs like this one by ZZ Top.

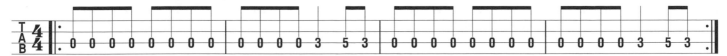

HIDE AWAY

First recorded in 1960 by Freddie King, this blues standard is a great example of the shuffle feel.

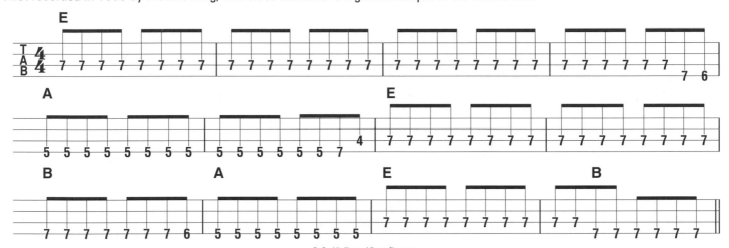

DETROIT ROCK CITY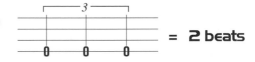

Now let's speed things up a little with a vintage rock classic by Kiss.

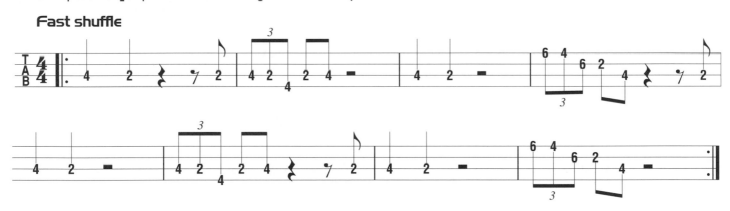

A **quarter-note triplet** divides two beats into three equal parts. For example, the three quarter notes in this triplet equal the same as two regular quarter notes.   = 2 beats

HOLD THE LINE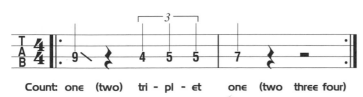

Observe the counting below the tab of this riff by the band Toto.

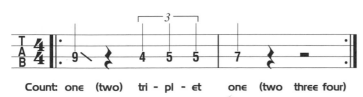

TRIPLET WALK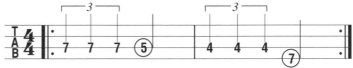

Before playing this next practice example, try tapping your foot with a steady, quarter-note pulse. Then, at the same time, say "tri-pl-et, tri-pl-et" with the quarter-note triplet rhythm. If you can do that, you've got it!

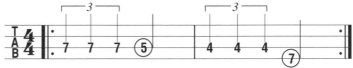

THE BOYS ARE BACK IN TOWN

Try playing this full song for more practice with triplets and the shuffle feel. On the original, classic recording by Thin Lizzy, the band tuned their instruments down a half step, but this recording is in standard tuning.

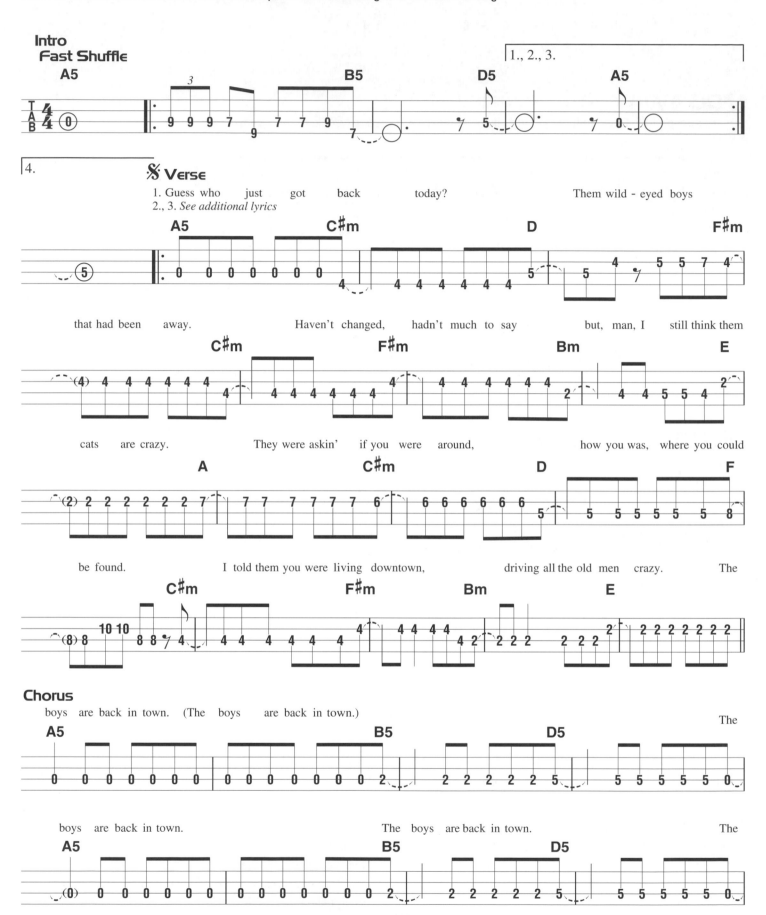

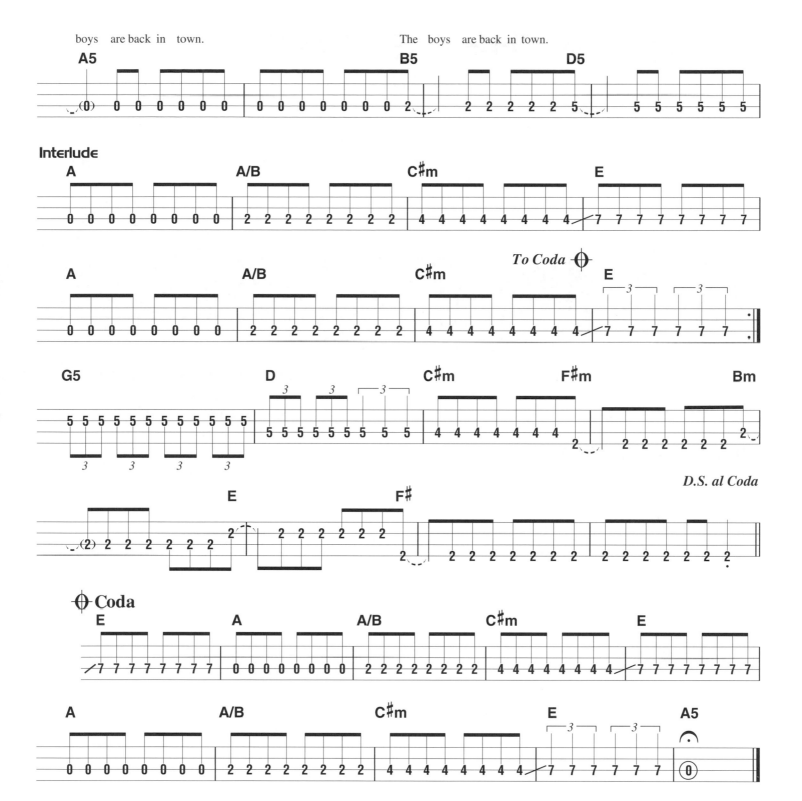

Additional Lyrics

2. You know that chick that used to dance a lot?
   Every night she'd be on the floor shakin' what she got.
   Man, when I tell you she was cool, she was red hot.
   I mean she was steamin'.
   And that time over at Johnny's place,
   Well, this chick got up and she slapped Johnny's face.
   Man, we just fell about the place.
   If that chick don't want to know, forget her.

3. Friday night they'll be dressed to kill
   Down at Dino's Bar and Grill.
   The drink will flow and blood will spill,
   And if the boys wanna fight, you better let 'em.
   That jukebox in the corner blasting out my favorite song.
   The nights are getting warmer, it won't be long.
   Won't be long till summer comes,
   Now that the boys are here again.

MOVIN' UP THE FRETBOARD: PART 2

Now that you've learned all of the notes within the first twelve frets, let's move on. Starting at fret 12, the entire note sequence repeats. In other words, fret 12 of the low E string has the same name as the open string (E), fret 13 has the same name as fret 1 (F), fret 14 is the same as fret 2, and so on. The notes above the 12th fret sound an octave above their lower counterparts. Let's take a look.

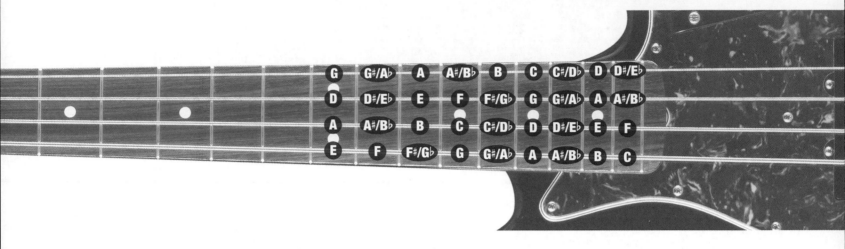

SWEET EMOTION

This bass intro from the band Aerosmith starts at the 12th fret of the A string. Begin with your 2nd finger and hold it there throughout the riff. Use your 3rd and 4th fingers for the G and A notes on the G string, respectively.

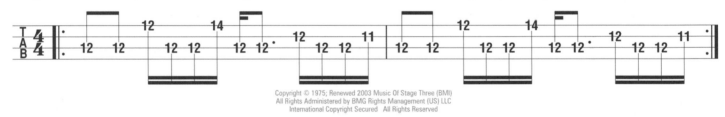

BY THE WAY

Here's another bass line by one of the most popular bassists in rock music, Flea of the Red Hot Chili Peppers. This one begins way up high on the neck. Once you reach the eighth measure you will see the instructions "D.C. al Fine," which means jump back to the beginning of the piece and end at the measure marked "Fine" (pronounced fee'-nay).

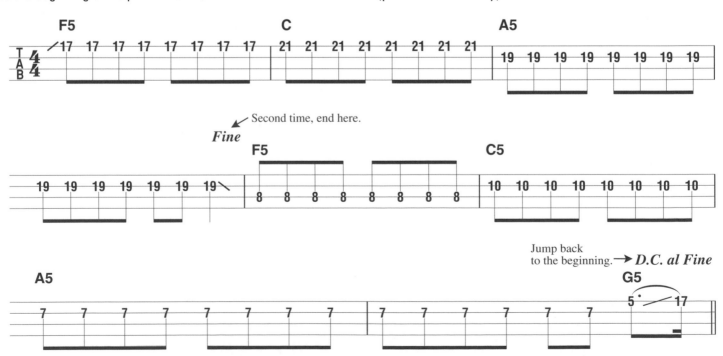

THE MAJOR SCALE

A **scale** is a group of notes ascending or descending in a specific order. In western music the most common scale is the **major scale**. It can be built starting on any root note, and follows a specific pattern of **whole steps** (2 frets) and **half steps** (one fret). The major scale includes one note each from the musical alphabet. Here it is beginning on the low E string.

E MAJOR SCALE

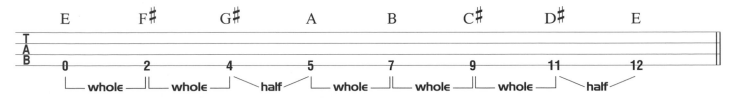

G MAJOR SCALE

Although it's easy to visualize the scale pattern along one string, it's not always practical to play it this way. The bass neck is a grid which makes it easy to memorize patterns or shapes. Every scale can be learned as a movable pattern of notes, and you can move that pattern anywhere on the neck to play the scale in any key. Here is the standard fingering for playing the major scale on the bass.

G MAJOR SCALE

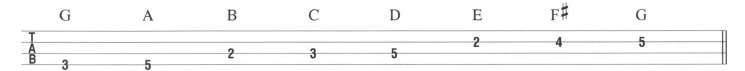

The scale above starts on the note G, so it's a G major scale. If you move the pattern to the A string and start on the note C it becomes a C major scale. If you move the pattern up two frets from C, it becomes a D major scale.

C MAJOR SCALE

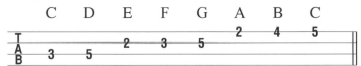

D MAJOR SCALE

Practicing scales is a great way to develop fret-hand dexterity. Start slowly, and gradually build up speed.

Here's another way to visualize the major scale pattern. The root is another word for the starting note of the scale.

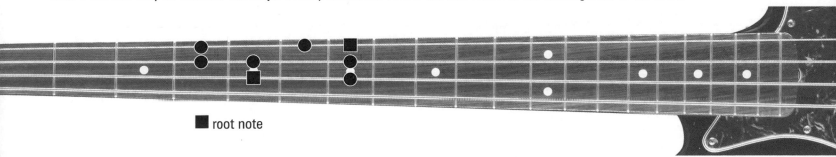

■ root note

The notes of the major scale are the foundation for countless melodies, bass lines, solos, and chord progressions. Here are some examples.

DO-RE-MI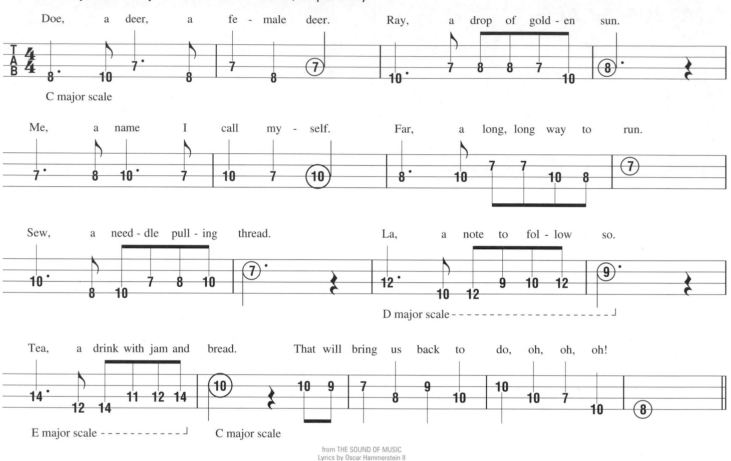

This song from *The Sound of Music* is one of the most famous uses of the major scale in popular music. The lyrics teach the seven solfege syllables commonly used to sing the major scale. The melody mostly consists of notes from the C major scale, and shifts to D major and E major in measures 11 and 13, respectively.

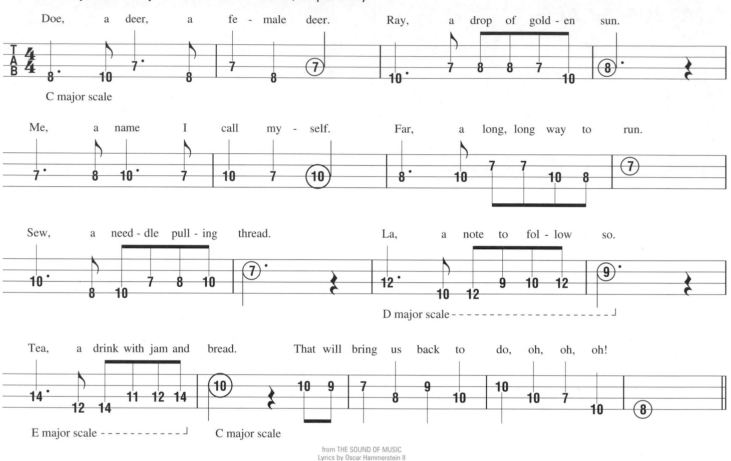

from THE SOUND OF MUSIC
Lyrics by Oscar Hammerstein II
Music by Richard Rodgers
Copyright © 1959 by Richard Rodgers and Oscar Hammerstein II
Copyright Renewed
Williamson Music, a Division of Rodgers & Hammerstein: an Imagem Company, owner of publication and allied rights throughout the world
International Copyright Secured   All Rights Reserved

JOY TO THE WORLD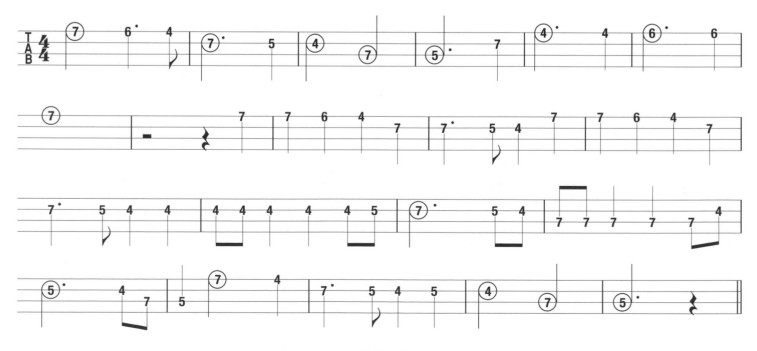

The melody of this famous Christmas carol, by Baroque composer George Frideric Handel, uses all of the notes in the D major scale.

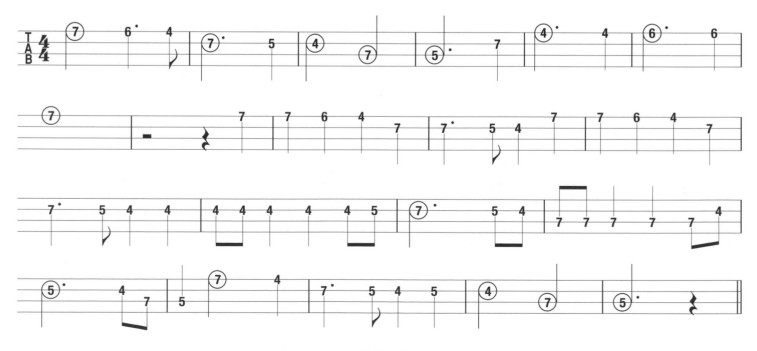

Words by Isaac Watts
Music by George Frideric Handel
Adapted by Lowell Mason
Copyright © 2016 by HAL LEONARD CORPORATION
International Copyright Secured   All Rights Reserved

MUSIC THEORY 101

When the notes of a song come from a particular scale, we say that the song is in the key of that scale. For example, if the notes of a song all come from the D major scale, we say that the song is in the key of D major.

LEAN ON ME

The intro to "Lean on Me" by Bill Withers uses notes exclusively from the C major scale, therefore it is in the key of C.

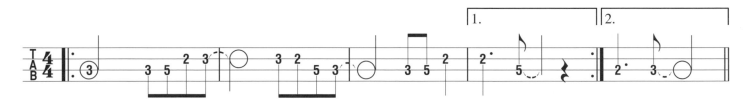

Notice how the bass line sounds "at rest" when you arrive at the last note (C)? This is because the C note is the root, or **tonic**—the note around which the key revolves.

MAJOR SCALE CHART

Major scales are the building blocks of music and music theory. Chords, chord progressions, and bass lines are all derived from scales. Here is a handy table that spells the notes in all 12 keys. Don't get bogged down trying to memorize it all at once, but you might want to dog-ear this page for future reference.

	1 (root)	2	3	4	5	6	7
C major	c	d	e	f	g	a	b
G major	g	a	b	c	d	e	f#
D major	d	e	f#	g	a	b	c#
A major	A	b	c#	D	E	f#	G#
E major	e	f#	G#	A	B	c#	D#
B major	B	c#	D#	E	f#	G#	A#
F# major	f#	G#	A#	B	c#	D#	E#
Db major	Db	Eb	F	Gb	Ab	Bb	C
Ab major	Ab	Bb	C	Db	Eb	F	G
Eb major	Eb	F	G	Ab	Bb	C	D
Bb major	Bb	C	D	Eb	F	G	A
F major	F	g	a	Bb	c	d	e

THE MINOR SCALE

Another common scale is the **natural minor scale**. Just like the major scale it can be built starting on any root note and follows a specific pattern of whole and half steps. Here it is beginning on E.

E MINOR SCALE

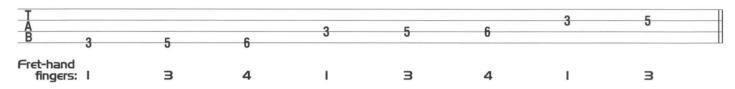

G MINOR SCALE

Here is the standard fingering and shape for playing a minor scale. We will start on the note G.

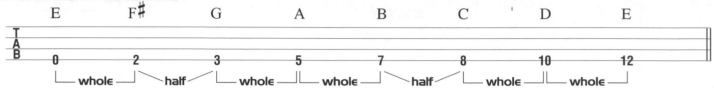

A MINOR SCALE/D MINOR SCALE

Now let's move it up two frets and start on A. After that, move up to the 3rd string and start on the root note D. The pattern remains the same when you move across these two strings.

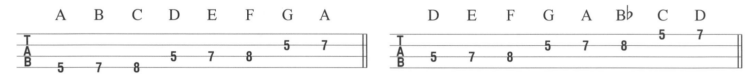

Here is another way to visualize the minor scale pattern.

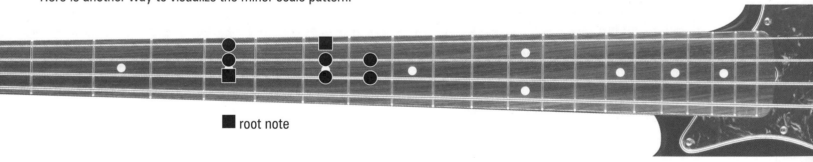

■ root note

ROCK LOBSTER 🔊

The C minor scale is in prominent use for the main riff of this fun and quirky B-52's song. Originally, this part was played on an electric guitar (tuned low), but it sounds great on bass too.

ROUNDABOUT

The E minor scale with the root on the open string retains the same pattern, except any note you would normally fret with the first finger is now an open string instead. Play this bass line by Chris Squire of Yes with a pick to execute the muted notes. Practice slowly!

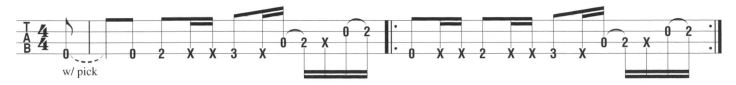

SMOOTH CRIMINAL

"Smooth Criminal" is from Michael Jackson's 1987 album *Bad*. The bass part uses four notes from the A minor scale: the root, 2nd, 3rd, and 7th. The 7th of the scale here (G) is played below the root note at the third fret, an octave below its place in the scale pattern.

DRIVE

Here is a song from R.E.M. The intro bass part is built from the D minor scale, which sounds great beneath the guitar's strummed D minor chord.

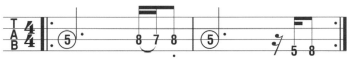

MAJOR AND MINOR TRIADS

A **triad** is a set of three notes from a scale—the root, 3rd, and 5th—that are used to form the basic **chords** a guitarist or pianist would play. While these instruments play the notes simultaneously for a chord, bassists play them separately and use the notes to create bass lines that support those chords.

All triads are labeled by their root note. The chord symbol "C" indicates a C major triad which is built from the root, 3rd, and 5th of the major scale.

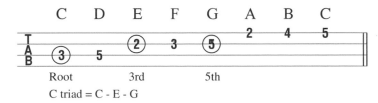

We can create a minor triad the same way by playing the root, 3rd, and 5th of the minor scale. Let's look at a C minor triad. All minor triads are labeled with the root and a lowercase "m" to indicate minor, for example: Cm.

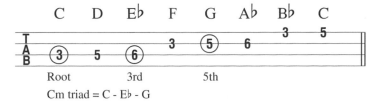

HOUND DOG 🔊

The bass line in this classic song made famous by Elvis Presley uses just a triad for each chord change until the tenth measure, where it walks down the F major scale to C.

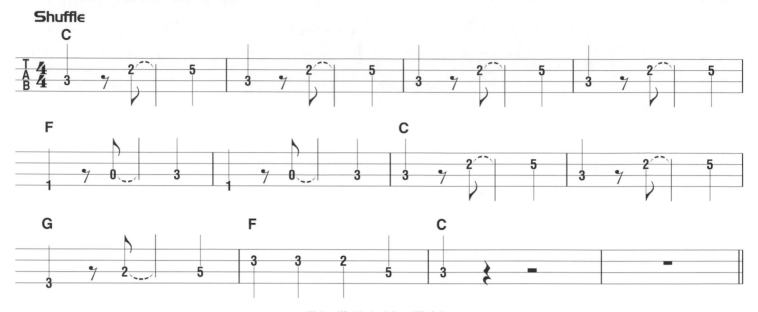

IN THE MIDNIGHT HOUR 🔊

In this song by Wilson Pickett, the bass line outlines a major triad for each E, A and B chord. Note the triad pattern starting on the open string for the E and A chords.

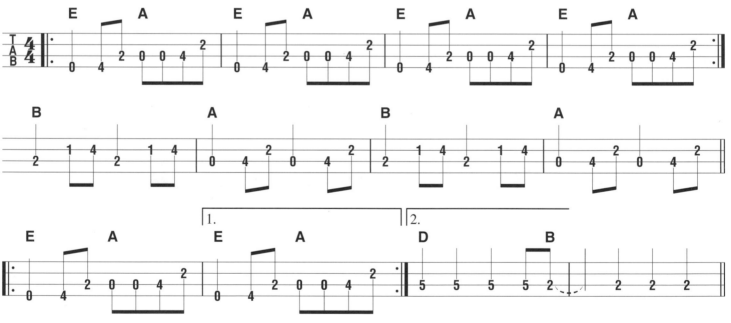

EIGHT DAYS A WEEK 🔊

"Eight Days a Week" is another great song by the Beatles. For the verse section, Paul McCartney outlines a triad over the G and E chords, but for the D he walks down using a root, 6th, 5th and 3rd from the D major scale.

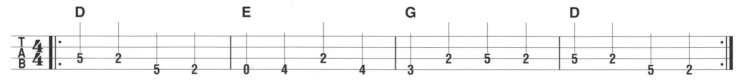

WHITE WEDDING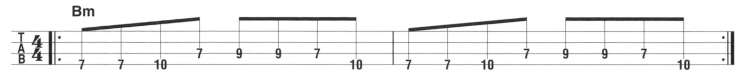

This classic Billy Idol song has a hypnotic bass line that centers on a B minor triad.

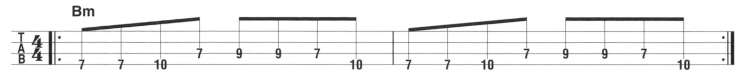

COME TOGETHER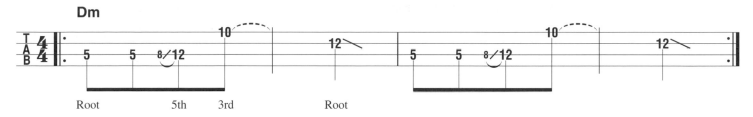

"Come Together" is the first track on the Beatles album *Abbey Road*. Its distinctive opening riff consists of only notes from the D minor triad. Instead of playing the low D on the 10th fret of the E string where the rest of the riff is positioned, Paul plays it at the A string's 5th fret, and slides up to the next note for a unique musical effect. Use your 3rd finger to slide up.

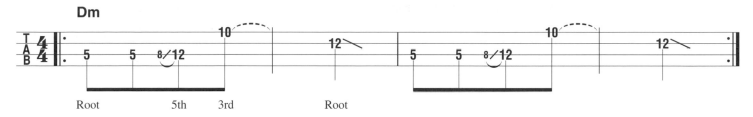

CREATING BASS LINES

Triads and scales are the building blocks of music, and knowing them is the key to creating bass lines. But how do you begin to use these tools to write your own bass parts?

START WITH THE ROOT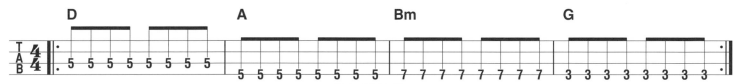

As bassists, our main job is to support the harmony (chords) of a song while also locking in with the rhythm. Sometimes all it takes to do the job right is to play the root notes of each changing chord. Some of the greatest songs have been played this way, including "With or Without You" by the band U2.

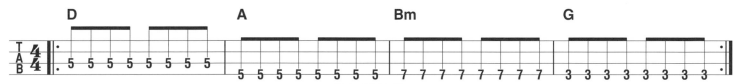

ADD THE FIVE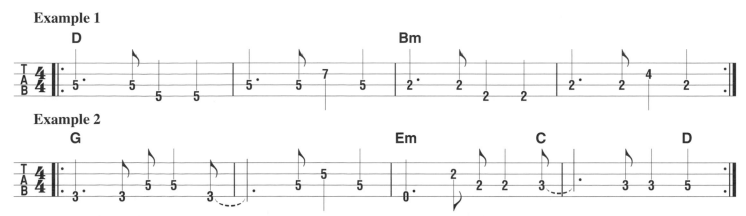

An absolute standard of bass lines is the root–5th pattern. Found in countless songs in all genres, this is a fool-proof way of creating a solid, functional line. Like the root-only approach above, this pattern moves to match each chord. Always place the root note on the first beat of each new chord.

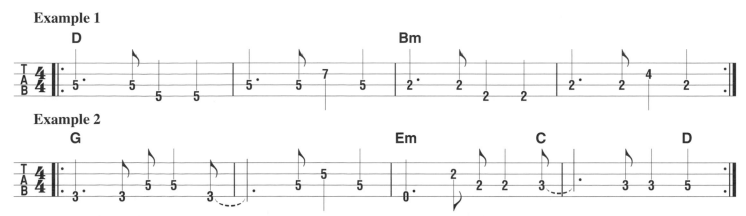

MIX IN A THIRD 🔊

Sometimes all a song needs is a root or root–5th line, and anything more would be superfluous. However, the addition of a third can create a different flavor. You may have noticed that the root–5th relationship stays the same regardless of whether the chord is major or minor. In contrast, we have to match the correct 3rd to the major or minor quality of the chord being played.

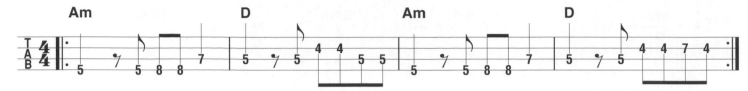

PASSING TONES 🔊

Up to this point, we've only used the notes of the triads to compose bass lines, and they are the most important notes we can use; they literally outline the chords other instruments are playing. We have more options, though, taking advantage of minor and major scales to find passing tones. These notes can help us bring a line smoothly from one chord to the next.

In "Orange Crush" by R.E.M., the F-sharp in the 2nd measure of the bass line acts as a passing tone from the Em chord to the G. Then in measure 3, the C acts as a passing tone from the 3rd of the G chord (B) to the root of the following D chord.

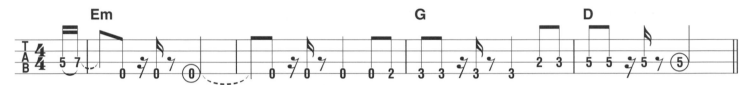

Using the concepts just described, try and create your own bass lines over the following chord progression.

JANGLY 🔊

Rhythm slashes like the ones in these measures tell the bass player they must improvise a part for the given chords. Play along with the audio backing track to experiment with creating your own bass lines.

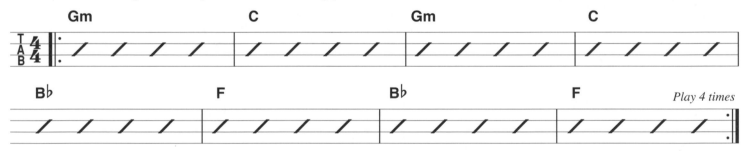

OTHER TIME SIGNATURES

All the song examples presented so far have been in the two most common meters: 4/4 and 3/4. These aren't the only time signatures in town, though. Let's explore a few more variations.

BLACK SUNSHINE 🔊

The "Black Sunshine" riff by White Zombie is in **6/4 time**. This means there are six beats in each measure, and a quarter note lasts one beat.

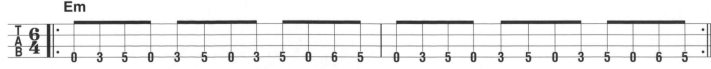

Count: one and two and three and four and five and six and

TAKE FIVE

This jazz favorite by Dave Brubeck is in **5/4 time**. For all time signatures, the top number of the fraction tells how many beats there are per measure, and the bottom number tells what kind of note equals one beat. So, one measure in this song has five quarter notes (five beats).

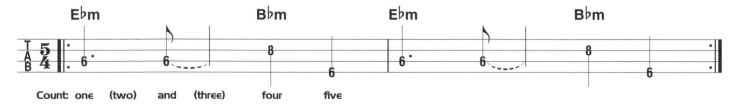

Count: one (two) and (three) four five

MONEY

"Money" is a song from the rock band Pink Floyd and is possibly the most recognizable riff in **7/4 time**. One measure in this tune has seven quarter notes (seven beats).

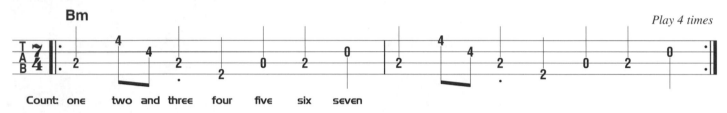

Count: one two and three four five six seven

A **6/8 time signature** means there are six beats in each measure, and an eighth note receives one beat. All note and rest values are proportionate to the eighth note. In other words, a quarter note receives two beats, a sixteenth note receives a half beat, and so on. In 6/8 time, the 1st and 4th beats are emphasized.

IRIS

"Iris" is a song by alternative rock band the Goo Goo Dolls.

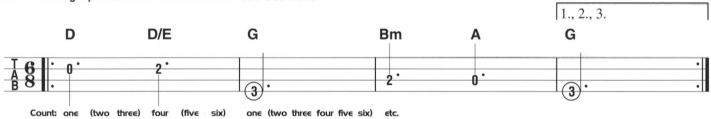

Count: one (two three) four (five six) one (two three four five six) etc.

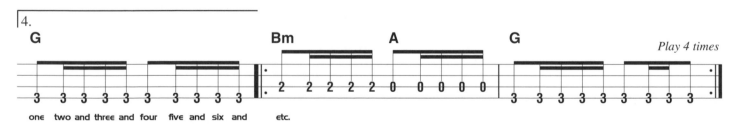

one two and three and four five and six and etc.

YOU'VE GOT TO HIDE YOUR LOVE AWAY

This song is another example of the Beatles' wonderful contribution to music. Notice the root–5th bass line on the C and D chords.

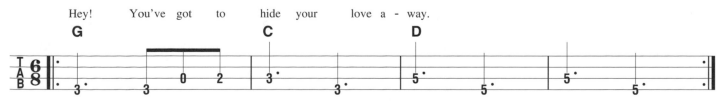

SLAP BASS

Slap bass is a popular technique for bass guitar that produces a percussive, rhythmic sound at the beginning of a note. To execute this technique, your thumb slaps against the lower strings to sound like a kick drum, and your index finger pulls on the higher strings to make a popping sound much like a snare.

Let's start with the **thumb slap**. Make a loose fist with your plucking hand and stick out your thumb like you're about to hitchhike [Photo 1]. Keep your hand in this shape and use the middle joint on your thumb to slap against the string [Photo 2]. The slap sound comes from the string hitting the metal frets where the neck meets the body of the bass. Keep your arm and wrist loose enough so that your thumb bounces back off the string after striking. This will allow the slapped note to sustain.

Photo 1

Photo 2

THUMBING

First, try to get a good slap sound with your thumb by playing slow quarter notes on the low E and A strings. When you feel a bit more confident with this new technique, try this rhythm. Use your fretting hand to dampen the string for the muted note and for rests.

YOU CAN CALL ME AL

"You Can Call Me Al" is a song by Paul Simon that features Bakithi Kumalo on bass.

LESSONS IN LOVE

Let's speed it up a little with this song by British musical group Level 42. This is a great workout for the thumb slap!

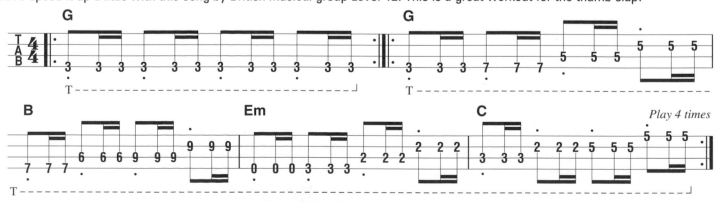

Once comfortable with the thumb slap, we can add the **finger pop**. Since the pop is an extension of the thumb slap, all you need to do is make a hook with your index finger to grab the string [Photo 3], pull up away from the fretboard [Photo 4] and release. When released, the string should snap back and hit the upper frets, creating the percussive pop sound. Use forearm movement when alternating between your thumb slapping down and your finger pulling up for the pop.

Photo 3

Photo 4

THANK YOU (FALLETINME BE MICE ELF AGAIN)

This is an R&B classic by Sly and the Family Stone. Their bass player, Larry Graham, was an early innovator of the slap style.

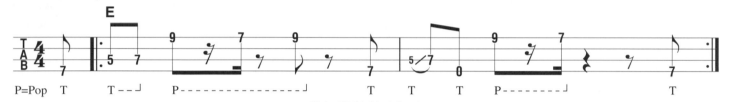

FLY AWAY

Earlier in this book, we played the chorus part of "Fly Away" by Lenny Kravitz. Here is the bass line for the verses. Try to combine the slap and pop as one fluid movement. This song uses a slight flange effect on the bass to get its signature, funky sound.

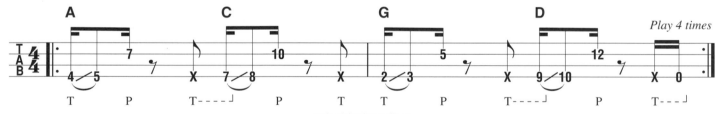

TREASURE

It's quite common for slap bass lines to include octaves, as this Bruno Mars song demonstrates. The octave shape lends itself to an alternating slap–pop motion.

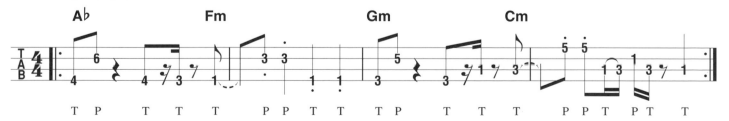

HIGHER GROUND

"Higher Ground" is a song written by Stevie Wonder in 1973. Close to 20 years later, the Red Hot Chili Peppers released a raucous cover version as the first single from their album *Mother's Milk,* featuring this great slap bass line.

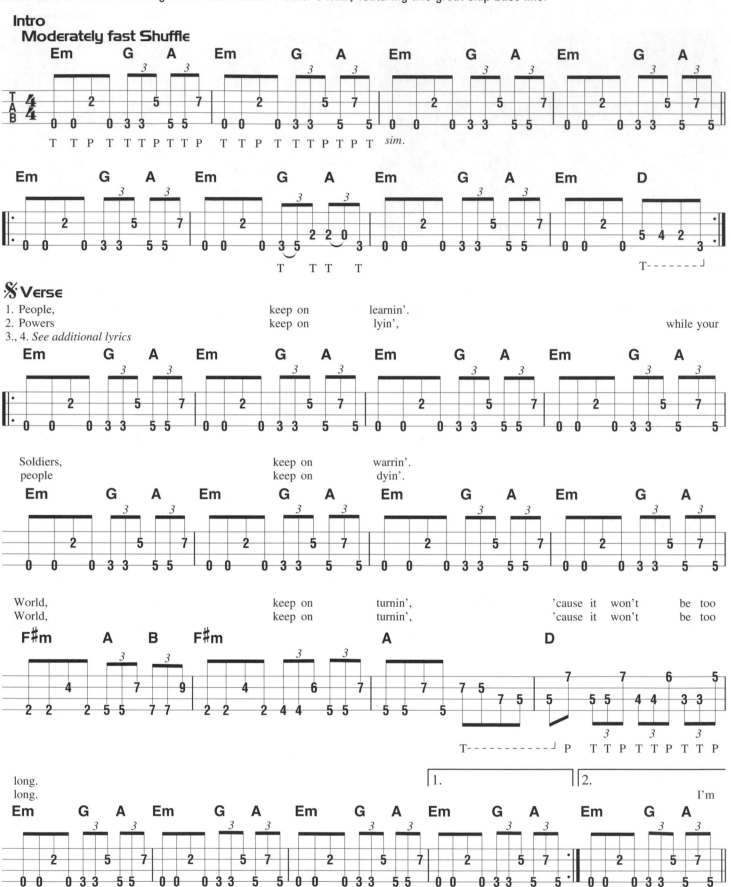

Chorus

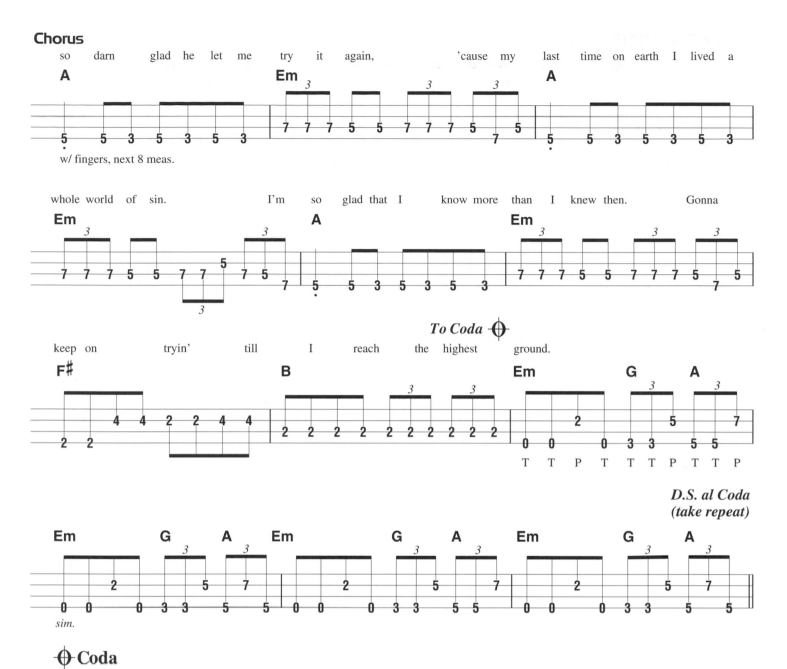

so darn glad he let me try it again, 'cause my last time on earth I lived a

w/ fingers, next 8 meas.

whole world of sin. I'm so glad that I know more than I knew then. Gonna

To Coda ⊕

keep on tryin' till I reach the highest ground.

D.S. al Coda
(take repeat)

sim.

⊕ Coda

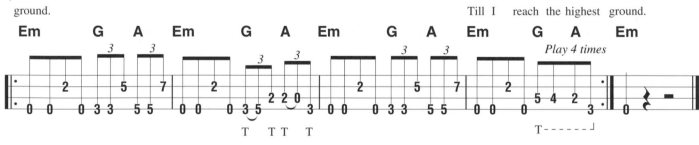

ground. Till I reach the highest ground.

Play 4 times

Additional Lyrics

3. Teachers, keep on teachin'.
   Preachers, keep on preachin'.
   World, keep on turnin',
   'Cause it won't be too long.

4. Lovers, keep on lovin'
   While believers keep on believin'.
   Sleepers, just stop sleepin'
   'Cause it won't be too long.

AEROPLANE

Let's finish with one more Red Hot Chili Peppers song excerpt. Flea is renowned for his great slap bass playing, and the verse section of "Aeroplane" is another superb example. In the chorus, when there's a slide down from the high G (10th fret), wait till beat 2 to begin the slide down.

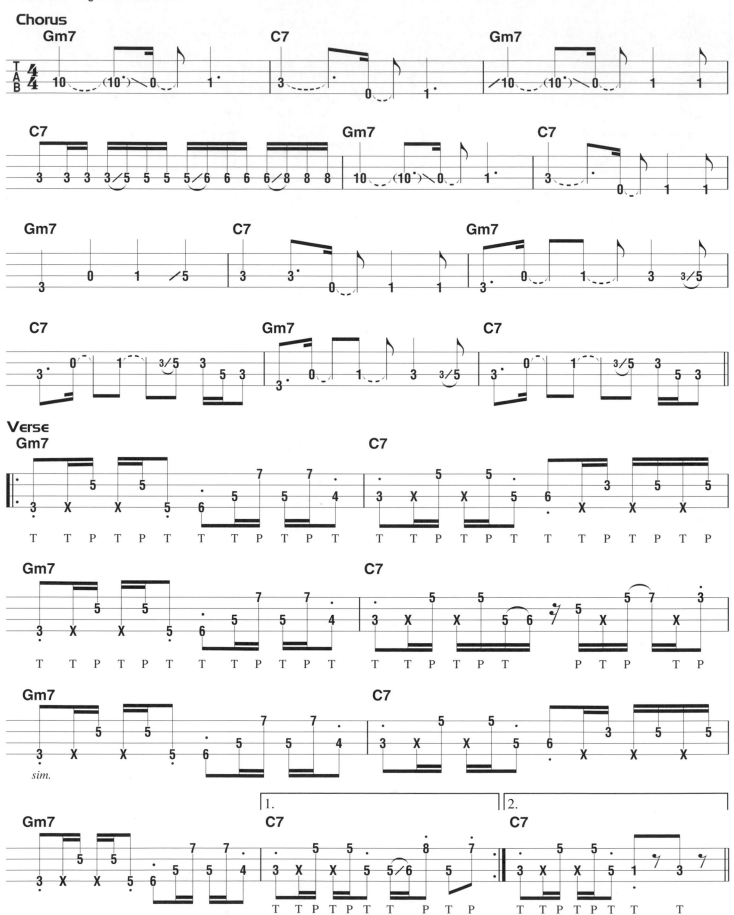

Words and Music by Anthony Kiedis, Flea, Chad Smith and David Navarro
© 1995 THREE POUNDS OF LOVE MUSIC
All Rights Reserved   Used by Permission